Beyond

Sameer Kamat is the founder of MBA Crystal Ball (www. mbacrystalball.com), an admissions consulting business that helps Indian candidates get into top business schools across the world.

He is active on several online discussion forums, where he provides free MBA and career advice to thousands of candidates struggling with questions and dilemmas addressed in this book.

Before embarking on the entrepreneurial journey, Kamat was a senior management professional in the corporate world with several years of international experience. He has managed multiple career changes (with and without an MBA) across information technology, consulting, finance (mergers & acquisitions) and finally, entrepreneurship.

Kamat completed his MBA from the University of Cambridge. He can be reached on info@mbacrystalball.com and on Twitter @mba_cb

PRAISE FOR THE BOOK

'Anybody who is intimidated by the prospect of stepping into the B-school jungle will find this book helpful.'
— *The Telegraph*

'Kamat systematically, and effectively, demolishes the notion that an MBA is a "magic wand that will change your life"... Refreshingly unlike any other business and management book...'
— *Mail Today*

'Kamat does a good job of explaining the finer points of getting in (to a B-school).'
— *Free Press Journal*

'A book that can set you on an effective path to sell yourself well.'
— *The Hindu Business Line*

Beyond the MBA Hype

A Guide to Understanding and Surviving B-Schools

SAMEER KAMAT

COLLINS BUSINESS
An Imprint of HarperCollins*Publishers*

First published in India in 2011 by Collins Business
An Imprint of HarperCollins *Publishers* India

Copyright © Sameer Kamat 2011, 2013

ISBN: 978-93-5029-078-1

8 10 9

Sameer Kamat asserts the moral right to be identified
as the author of this book.

The views and opinions expressed in this book are the author's
own and the facts are as reported by him, and the publishers are
not in any way liable for the same.

HarperCollins *Publishers*

A-75, Sector 57, Noida, Uttar Pradesh 201301, India
1 London Bridge Street, London, SE1 9GF, United Kingdom
2 Bloor Street East, Toronto, Ontario M4W 1A8, Canada
Lvl 13, 201 Elizabeth Street (PO Box A565, NSW, 1235), Sydney
NSW 2000, Australia
195 Broadway, New York, NY 10007, USA

Typeset in 11.5/14.5 Adobe Minion Pro
Jojy Philip, New Delhi 110 015

Printed and bound at
Thomson Press (India) Ltd.

Contents

Acknowledgements

Going by the assumption that the bookies won't be betting heavily on this book winning a Pulitzer or a Booker any time soon, I'll take this opportunity to thank a few special people.

God (no, not Sachin Tendulkar, but the original One) for bestowing on me all the resources and opportunities in a world where both are considered tough to come by.

My parents for giving me an education (formal and informal) that helped me explore unconventional opportunities beyond the traditional, time-tested 'best practices' that kids from modest backgrounds are expected to adopt.

My wife Swati and my daughter Alisha for providing a solid support system throughout the journey.

The entire Judge Business School family (my classmates, professors, administrative team and others that I interacted with) at the University of Cambridge, where I had a truly transformational experience.

The HarperCollins India team – Krishan Chopra and Amit Agarwal – for polishing the initial draft and converting it into a high quality product.

My agents Jayapriya Vasudevan and Priya Doraswamy from Jacaranda.

Jeevan Subramaniam, executive managing editor, Berrett-Koehler, for being my sounding board and giving me precious inputs on the publishing industry.

All the MBA candidates who have shared their stories with me. If any of the incidents sound unusually familiar, don't be surprised, it just might be your story.

▶ ACKNOWLEDGEMENTS

All the others who I have not been able to list down here due to reasons that fluctuate somewhere between word-count constraints and my diminishing cognitive abilities.

Preface

As a computer science engineering graduate, I was happily settled in my role as an engagement manager with IBM. The salary and the designation were both good. And working for a strong brand meant that social prestige came automatically. International assignments provided plenty of travel opportunities. But there was still something amiss. Despite the variety I had when it came to clients, industries, locations and teams, the whole project cycle was becoming monotonous and predictable.

After about a decade of experience, I was on the other (non-flattering) side of thirty and I had about three more decades of productive working years to navigate before retirement. To secure my future, straightforward solutions like job-hopping for a higher salary were not the best way forward. For I knew that sooner or later, I'd be in the exact same position that I was trying to get away from.

That's when I hit the Internet and started researching. An MBA seemed like a good option. But it seemed too good to be true. There were a lot of 'what-if' queries in my mind. What if I don't get into a good programme? What if I don't do well with so many super-intelligent candidates competing against one another? What if I don't get a good internship? What if I don't get a good job? What if I'm not able to repay my huge education loan? So I researched more. And the confusion grew.

Also, I was not the typical candidate for an American MBA programme. I was much older, married and had a daughter – a family man.

I needed to shortlist programmes where I would fit in well and not look like a freak. I wanted a small yet diverse programme that placed emphasis on collaboration as opposed to cut-throat competition. Most importantly, I knew that five, ten or twenty years later, what would stick to me wouldn't be the academic concepts or the MBA frameworks, but the brand. Call me superficial, but I guessed (and I still feel the same way today) that the corporate world places a great deal of importance on brands. You are who you have been associated with. Whether that's good or bad, I don't want to judge. But it's worked for me, so far. So I'm more than happy with my decision.

I gathered that the quality of education you'd get from most good schools would be good. They all use similar textbooks, case studies and projects. The professors are there to facilitate the knowledge transfer and can't magically transform mediocre students into geniuses. The teaching methodology may differ and a lot depends on the students' capacity to absorb what is thrown at them. I realized B-schools were more of a filtering ground, so I'd be alright if I stuck to schools where the filtering criteria were the most stringent. And I chose the University of Cambridge.

I was taking a big enough risk by leaving my comfort zone. I guess I was just playing safe by sticking to a brand that had been around for ages.

I can't say what I did was right or perfect. I can't say that what worked for me will work for everyone else. All I can say is that I worked out a strategy after a lot of introspection and stuck to the game plan till the very end.

In hindsight, I feel I was lucky and privileged to have been part of an exceptional MBA programme at the University of Cambridge. I got an excellent education, made some fantastic friends from thirty-one countries, took a calculated risk and followed my intuition to take up a job in India immediately after completing my MBA (this was before the recession, so it was more out of choice than necessity). I had the opportunity to work in one of the most coveted post-MBA fields – mergers and acquisitions. But I am also aware that the entire story could have ended up in a totally different direction. I'm not going to pretend to be a super-confident, all-knowing oracle who knows this topic inside out. If many of the sections in this book sound a little ambiguous and uncertain, I know I'm still striking a chord with many readers who are feeling exactly the same right now – paranoid and unsure.

Since the time I completed my MBA in 2005, the dynamics have changed in several areas. There's more competition to get into good schools, there are several new B-schools that have mushroomed across the globe, the course fees have gone through the roof, the economy is more uncertain than ever, the job market is going through turmoil. In short, the stakes are much higher now. Any decision you take can have an amplified impact on your future.

Many of the fears, apprehensions that I personally experienced during my MBA ride were not justified. I was fully aware of this fact. But that did not stop me from pushing my nervous system into overdrive during my decision-making process. I would devour any information that I could get my hands on. Whether this information came from blogs, discussion forums, official websites or word-of-mouth was immaterial. My need for information needed to be satiated. Period. If you are in a similar situation, you'll find this book helpful.

Introduction

Indians, specially the ambitious ones, have never had it easy. Be it any field – career, education, business, marriage, sports, acquiring wealth – there is one thing you can be sure of: competition. Loads of it, actually.

Take education, for instance. It started off at the pre-primary stage when your parents struggled to get you into the best nursery in the city. If you really look back with an objective lens, your parents' educational background, financial health and recommendations from the local MLA should have had nothing to do with you getting a seat in there. But for some reason, it did. The roly-poly kid sharing the desk with you probably didn't know it either. But the fact that his equally roly-poly parents drove into school for the admission interview in their brand new BMW, sauntered into the principal's office in their branded clothes and spoke Queen's English (strangely, in an American accent) during the interview, did play a role in influencing the decision.

Fortunately for you (or unfortunately, if you consider the broader philosophical perspective), your folks faced the brunt of the competition then and you were let off relatively scot-free. However, somewhere along your journey through primary school, you realized that the burden of tackling competition was essentially your headache, a chronic one that neither Zandu balm nor any of the other trusted off-the-shelf desi alternatives could fix. Exams, graded assignments and projects became an integral part of growing up.

Still, in school, the competition was limited to your classmates. Then things got bigger and worse – competitive public examinations took the entire game to a whole new level. The magnitude changed dramatically – from sixty students in a class to several lakh students competing fiercely to get into the top engineering, medical and management institutions. Our very own IITs and IIMs highlight this contrast effectively.

When it comes to competitive entrance tests for management colleges, the Common Admission Test (CAT) is the undisputed king. The scale and reach of the Graduate Management Admission Test (GMAT), a standardized test that is generally the first hurdle to cross when it comes to international school admissions, is smaller. Between 2008 to 2012, the number of Indian residents taking the GMAT went up from around 19,000 to 23,000.[1] In contrast, in 2012, close to two lakh candidates took the CAT in India.[2] That makes the domestic CAT market ten times bigger than that for GMAT. No wonder our desi coaching institutions go gaga over it and shower all their attention and resources to CAT training and coaching. Students hopeful of getting into the top Indian business schools flock to these CAT coaching classes. Not all of them are successful, though. There's a huge demand-supply gap out there. At the time of writing this book, there are ten IIMs, with several more in the pipeline. The functioning IIMs can only offer around 3,000 seats. The institutions ranked after the IIMs accept another 15,000 to 20,000 candidates. These include institutions like XLRI, Jamshedpur; Faculty of Management Studies, New Delhi; Jamnalal Bajaj Institute of Management Studies, Mumbai; National Institute of Industrial Engineering (NITIE), Mumbai; Narsee Monjee Institute of Management Studies, Mumbai; Management Development Institute (MDI), Gurgaon; and S.P. Jain Institute of Management and Research, Mumbai.

Beyond the credible ones that have built their reputation and track record over time, there are numerous other institutions

[1] GMAC 2012 Asian Geographic Trend Report for GMAT Examinees.
[2] *The Times of India*, 9 January 2013.

in India that offer MBA programmes. An estimated 1.5 lakh students attend such B-schools every year. Many of them pay a lot of money, but end up with a paper degree that has no educational or market value.

So what do you do after the CAT results come out and you fall in the not-so-fortunate category? For starters, think if you want to settle for some mediocre option. Or take some time off and then start looking at the international MBA scene. If you have scored a decent percentile[3] in the CAT exam, chances are you'll score well in the GMAT as well. That opens up a world of opportunities in the international business school circuit. At a very rough estimate, if you score above the 80 percentile in CAT, then it is pretty much possible (with the right study material and the right amount of practice) for you to get a GMAT score in the 650-750 range, which makes you competitive for the international top 100 MBA programmes.

Thus for many Indian candidates looking for quality management education, the story doesn't end with their CAT results. For those who view the MBA degree as a long-term investment, the game has just begun. As the joke goes, the top talent from India that can't get into the IIMs settles for Harvard, Stanford, Wharton, and the rest of the top programmes globally. Those who say that aren't being arrogant (well, maybe some are). Their comments are just reflecting the statistical reality in a country like India. Fantastic talent minus the resources to match.

This is also where the fun starts. Despite the competition, the analytical skills and the immense potential of our people, most

[3] A percentile score indicates the candidate's relative position vis-à-vis other test-takers. For instance, a candidate with a 90 percentile score would mean 90 per cent of the total test-takers have scores below this candidate. A 'percentage', in contrast, is an absolute value and provides no indication of how many folks scored higher than or less than that value.

MBA | Indian MBA |

ears for American programmes, 30 years for European MBA | Median age: 22 years |

ualification: 16 years of undergraduate education;[4] Graduate (mostly engineers, CAs)[5] | Pre-MBA qualification: Graduate (BEngg, CA, BSc, BCom, BBA, etc.) and Postgraduate (MSc, MCom, MA, etc.) |

Exam | GMAT (+ TOEFL for English proficiency) | Varied: Common Admission Test (CAT); Symbiosis National Aptitude Test (SNAP); |

ng now, as applicants from other streams are getting more interested in international MBA options.

Topic	International MBA	Indian MBA
	Maximum applicants from US; 2nd biggest applicant pool: India	XLRI Admission Test (XAT); Management Aptitude Test (MAT) conducted by All India Management Association (AIMA); Narsee Monjee Management Aptitude Test (NMAT), plus over 50 more institute-specific tests
B-school Selection Process	Importance given to 'fit' with the B-school (industry/role specialization, post-MBA career options, etc.)	Concept of 'fit' doesn't exist. Reputation of the B-school is the primary criteria
	Considerable research needed to shortlist B-schools. Everyone doesn't apply to Harvard	By virtue of taking the CAT exam, everyone is considered an applicant to the IIMs
Admission Process	Equal importance to entrance exam (GMAT), essays (the number varies from 3-10+), recommendations (2), CV, interview	Predominantly entrance test-based. Other components (group discussion/ interview) also included, but the entrance exam has a very high cut-off
Programme Duration	US – 2 years Europe, Asia, Australia, Canada – 1 year	India – 2 years

Topic	International MBA	Indian MBA
Cost	1 year programme: Rs 30 lakh	2 year programme: Rs 5–20 lakh
	2 year programme: Rs 40–75 lakh	
Typical Class Profile	Highly diverse: multiple nationalities, industries, roles & functions	Homogenous: Single nationality, mainly technical (like IT) backgrounds
Teaching Styles	Case studies, lectures, group studies, relatively greater emphasis on practical aspects. More interactive, experience-sharing among peers	Similar mix, but as there is little real-world experience in the class to tap into, the learning can become theoretical
Recruitment Process	Independent initiative by students, B-school plays minimal role	B-school gets most students placed through on-campus placements
Post-MBA Careers	Lateral placements, that is, pre-MBA skills & capabilities leveraged	Fresher-level jobs, that is, pre-MBA experience effectively irrelevant

This book focuses primarily on Indian candidates considering international MBA options. We will also talk about the typical issues, challenges and dilemmas Indian applicants grapple with when it comes to international MBA programmes.

There are numerous challenges associated with the MBA rigmarole and some of them have nothing to do with competition at all. Due to lack of awareness or otherwise, candidates set the expectation levels too high – from the business school, course content and final degree. A major chunk of this book is dedicated to addressing that expectation mismatch. The key message here is: if you approach it with the right attitude, expectation and perspective, you've already won half the battle.

1 Why Go for an MBA?

ONCE UPON A TIME

Let's set the ball rolling with the heart-warming, soul-stirring story of two buddies – Santa and Banta. On second thoughts, considering these are the two most common names in our pop culture, let's think of some realistic ones. How about Sachin Nimbalkar and Mitendra (Mitu) Lamba?

Like most other students in India, Mitu and Sachin stuck to the traditional career options, and graduated as engineers in Information Technology (IT). Now for many engineering graduates, moving directly into management education is a popular option to broaden their focus and move out of technical roles. That's what happened with Mitu and Sachin. They had just completed their engineering degrees in Information Technology, tried their best to crack the IIM entrance examination, and failed. Their entrance exam scores, though good, weren't considered good enough by schools such as Faculty of Management Studies, Delhi; Institute of Foreign Trade, Delhi; Institute of Rural Management, Anand; or S.P. Jain Institute of Management and Research, Mumbai. 'I'm not going to take up a software development job,' Mitu was clear in his head. 'It's so passé. MBA it shall be.'

Both of them had job offers from leading software companies that had come to their engineering college for campus recruitment. Sachin had made up his mind to take up the offer. Mitu had other plans, for his rich businessman father had given him an ultimatum: 'Do what you want to do for the next five years. Studies, job…in India, abroad…I don't care. After that I need you back here, running the empire I've created.' Mitu had nodded obediently, but in his mind he wanted to get out of India, away from all this. He was going to need some help.

'Axe-pert Consultants' (*pyaar se log humein 'AC' kehte hain*; people affectionately call us 'AC') were the most visible players in the international educational consulting space in Delhi. Their website had super-happy faces of satisfied clients with super-cool testimonials. 'Myself Parminder. Without help from the axeperts at AC, I wouldn't be in the Munich attending the bestest MBA programme in the whole wide world!' AC's advertising budget appeared to be inexhaustible. They were everywhere – on Internet sites, on the local cable TV, in newspapers. 'Considering they spend so much on ads, they must be good,' thought Mitu. He fixed up an appointment with them to gain some more clarity about the process. Cost wasn't a problem as he knew his dad would fund the entire thing.

At the AC office, Mitu had an hour-long meeting with a counsellor, Reema, and returned home super-charged. She had given him several options to choose from, including some universities he'd never heard of, but again he wasn't the 'axepert', Reema was, right? The best part of the deal – an admission guarantee and assured scholarships. They'd also help out with documentation and the rest of the formalities, with visa, ticketing, yada yada. The total damages – a few lakh rupees. Hardly a dent in the Lamba clan's finances.

An excited Mitu shared his story with Sachin, who didn't seem impressed. 'I don't know, man. Maybe I'm being paranoid. But something just doesn't seem right with this whole approach. What about the selection process? What about GMAT? What about essays?' Sachin had read up on the selection process for some of the well-known schools and was a little more aware about the hurdles candidates were required to clear.

'*Abe phattu*...you've always shied away from risks in life. If you won't take risks, you'll never get anywhere in life. You don't want to retire as a software programmer, do you?' a defiant Mitu retorted. 'No, I don't. But neither do I want to take knee-jerk reactions. Calculated risks are fine, but this would be plain stupid. It can't be that simple, right?' Sachin bristled.

'Reema told me these schools don't require a GMAT. And they'll manage the rest of the process for me. Why worry about entrance exams, essays when you can take a short cut and take the flight out? They charge a lot for all this, you know. And if they are willing to do some leg-work on my behalf, what's wrong with that?'

'It's not a low-skilled job that you are applying for, mere *bhai*. You can't expect them to do your job for you. What about the quality of teaching there? Placements? What about...?'

'You are just being jealous, dude. Suit yourself. Fix that bug in your code. I've got bigger plans. I'll send you postcards from Sydney...or Amsterdam...or I don't know...some exotic place.'

But destiny had other plans for Mitu. He decided not to sign up with Axepert Consulting. 'Saved by a whisker, dude,' he had exclaimed when he met Sachin a few days after his discussion with Reema from AC. 'I met up with this guy at the party. He was one of the "satisfied" clients who got his beaming mugshot plastered on the AC website. He says he was taken for a ride.'

'What do you mean?' Sachin was curious. 'They took his application money and ran away?'

'Worse! They stayed back and sent him abroad to this godforsaken university. A complete waste of time, money and effort, according to the bloke. Says he'd have been better-off doing what he was doing in India. The degree, paper degree rather, was worthless there and it's worthless here. The employers in phoren-land didn't want to touch him. So he's back home doing exactly what he was doing three years back.'

'Scary! Close shave, indeed, Mitu. So what's the plan now?' Sachin wanted to know if the unplanned shock therapy had worked on his friend.

'Well, dad wants me to join him in the family business. But if I get into it right now, I don't think I'd ever be able to convince him to allow me to pursue a good MBA programme from a legit university after a few years. Then they'll start pestering me to get "settled", you know how it goes, marriage and stuff. So I'm thinking of taking up the software role, though I know that's not what I want to do for the rest of my life. Maybe I'll spend a few years there and try the MBA option again after that.'

'Yeah, logical choice. Can't argue with that line of thinking,' Sachin smiled, happy for his friend.

Now, let's stop our elaborate plot and get down to real business. Over the past several decades, various players that make up the MBA industry have left no stone unturned to convince us that this degree can change our lives for the better. They have made it seem like a magic pill that will end all our woes and travails. The overdose of optimism that we all get bombarded with does more harm than good for it raises expectations to impractical levels.

This book will give you a behind-the-scenes look at each stage of your application process, the MBA course itself and what you can expect after you graduate. You will become aware of aspects that many official websites and published material stay away from (or intentionally hide?), but which are absolutely critical for you to be cognizant about before you decide to take the plunge.

The following chapters will highlight many of the good, bad and ugly facets of business education. Based on your own current situation and your personal goals, you can interpret the content from each chapter differently. Analyse your reactions as you think about the best- and worst-case scenarios. By the time you reach the end of this book, you'd hopefully have developed a personalized roadmap for yourself.

Let's take it one step at a time, starting with the basic reasons you would want to start thinking seriously about an MBA degree abroad.

PRIMARY MOTIVATIONS

Most students who have not already joined a postgraduation degree (in India or abroad) put their further education aspirations on the backburner and join the corporate world, just like Mitu and Sachin did. After his half-baked efforts to fly out of the country and join an MBA programme flopped, Mitu took up the software job that he was so reluctant to accept initially. But the desire to complete an MBA degree was still dormant somewhere in there as he went through the regular 9-to-5 grind at work.

'Why do you want an MBA degree?' is one question you'd hear several times after you announce to the world at large about your intentions. Friends, relatives, employers and colleagues would want to know what got into you to throw away a 'perfectly good job' and chase a new dream. So you'd better have a few convincing sounding reasons ready in your arsenal.

The IT industry used to be a hot destination till about a decade ago. Engineering colleges increased their IT student capacity. Then, after going through a boom-and-bust phase (dotcom era, recession, outsourcing bans, etc.), though the industry still employs a lot of fresh graduates, it isn't the dream destination it once was. Many IT employees, especially those working in large companies with pyramidal hierarchies, start complaining of stagnation and lack of growth as early as one to two years into the job. There are too many people at the base of the pyramid and they perceive the vertical journey to be too slow, with hardly any growth options for the next four to five years. With the number of outsourced projects dwindling and the 'bench' (those who aren't assigned to live projects) size increasing, junior employees such as Mitu don't seem to have the patience to wait for the tough phase to get over.

The story in other industries isn't very different. Fresh engineers who have joined in technical roles start getting the feeling that they could get meatier roles with an MBA. Others feel it's an easy way to settle and work abroad, with prospects of better roles, better pay and a better life.

But let's get back to Mitu's story, who started viewing the MBA as an escape route, without really knowing where it could or should take him.

After three years in the software company, Mitu's desire to move out of the role was stronger than ever. His general response to the 'Why MBA' question was, 'Well, I think I've reached a roadblock now. I need some time to think about what I want to do in my career, and I can't possibly sit at home twiddling my thumbs or worse, get pulled in by my dad into the family business. An MBA seems like a good option. It'll give me the space and the time to introspect and figure out the answers.' This response, though perfectly logical to Mitu, might be interpreted by B-school admissions committees as a lethal combination of dazzling ignorance and profound philosophical insights.

Whether you decide to be diplomatic (especially with employers) or straightforward is up to you. It is likely that your answer may overlap with some of the points listed below.

Career

We associate good designations with prestige, status and power. The journey from the bottom of the food chain to the top is often slow and painful. Many employees start feeling stagnant in their jobs. Over the years, for many, the job profile does not change and their day-to-day routines become monotonous and mechanical. There is a lack of variety in what they do, with little possibility of any substantial change in their job profiles in the near term (or even in the long term). An MBA degree can change that.

For people in operational or support roles and especially for those in the junior or mid-level roles, there may be a feeling that their roles lack real responsibility as they are unable to be part of critical decision-making processes within the organization. The top-brass within the firm takes the decisions that are followed by the line staff without any questions. Again, an MBA degree could help them change their career profile.

In addition to a vertical jump in their current designations, an MBA degree can often lead to a change of function, industry or geography (or all three).

Change of function: An Information Technology (IT) support engineer may want to move into a software development role. An accountant from the audit team may find the frequent travel exhausting and try for a role in the treasury department in corporate finance. An operations guy working in commissioning of heavy engineering equipment may want to move into a commercial role.

Change of industry: The high-flying management consultant hoping for a better work-life balance may want to move into a regular industry role within a manufacturing firm. The store manager working in the retail industry could look at the real estate market. The research analyst in the credit department of a multinational company may try to enter the investment banking industry.

Change of geography: Quite a few professionals from India get a chance to work on international projects for time periods varying from a few months to several years. In the good ol' days, the IT industry used to provide plenty of such opportunities. Many of these folks deputed onsite would never return. The land of opportunity provided options too tempting to resist.

However, these opportunities are dwindling now as there's a greater focus on offshore development, as opposed to the infamous practice of 'body-shopping' that was prevalent earlier. So, many professionals look at a top MBA as a way to tap into the international opportunities. The forex trader on Dalal Street may want to experience life in the fast lane on Wall Street. The marketing professional in Delhi may want to experience life on the US West Coast for a few years. The Chennai-based manufacturing consultant could think about relocating to China for a few years to experience the frenetic pace of activity and the world-class manufacturing processes she's read so much about.

Knowledge

Undergraduate and specialized professional degrees have a focused approach to knowledge. An engineer will focus more on technical aspects than on economics, marketing or accounting. An accountant, on the other hand, will focus more on money than on strategy or operations. And though there are bound to be exceptions, not many would argue with that logic.

Given that organizations do not work in silos, there is considerable interaction across functions within and outside the organization. The accountant from the previous example, though ultimately responsible for the accounting department only, would still have to deal with people from the operational divisions, the HR team, customers, Information Technology (IT) department and senior management. For this interaction to happen smoothly, an understanding of the underlying concepts in various other areas will be imperative and will make a substantial difference to the accountant's productivity and efficiency.

Even after one starts working, the focus rarely shifts away from the core qualifications. Some companies have structured jobrotation as part of their company policy. This allows employees to move across departments and functions after pre-defined time periods. These are, however, exceptions to the rule as frequent internal rotations can prove expensive to the company, and not just from a financial angle. The rotated employee has to go through the learning curve all over again in the new role. It also means the organization can't tap into three years spent in learning the ropes in the previous role.

An MBA could offer a good platform to gain new skills and techniques and fill in the theoretical and technical gaps.

Network

If you've heard about (and believe in) the concept of six degrees of separation, you are probably convinced that you can reach any person in the world by approaching someone you know, who knows someone else and so on, in six steps. If you could do this in six steps without an MBA, you could possibly accomplish the same in three or four steps with a high-powered MBA under your belt.

In the business world, your Rolodex is your magic wand. At least that's the general perception. Your powerful connections earn you respectability in your domain. You know you can call up that close friend (who by the way is also a top-shot businessman or politician) and request for a favour.

What most of the blue- and white-collared staff often lack is this network. Many have perfected the art of name-dropping as a quick, painless and low-calorie-burning option to gain credibility. And you cannot name-drop unless you have a big list of names to begin with. The higher the exclusivity of the list, the better the impact. The jaw-dropping effectiveness of name-dropping, unfortunately, hasn't been proven scientifically, and it all depends on the image of the name-dropper.

Second MBA Degree

Several candidates who already have an MBA from one of the Indian business schools apply to international MBA programmes for a second MBA degree. This situation might seem unusual in other parts of the world, but it's quite typical for Indian applicants. Our conventional two-year MBA programmes take in candidates with little or no experience. Most students go on for their post-graduate studies (irrespective of whether it's in a technical area or in the management field) immediately after completing their basic graduation. So the entire education chapter gets closed before they decide to hit the working world. And it's been a time-tested approach in India for several decades now.

However, for many professionals, especially those who have been working in international organizations, the feeling of discomfort starts after a few years. They start getting the nagging impression that they've 'outgrown' their earlier degrees, and that these cannot help them move forward. They see that their colleagues, counterparts in other countries or business partners have impressive credentials. Though it isn't openly mentioned, for senior-level promotions, international or domestic growth opportunities, those with an international degree seem to get some brownie points. The global recession has triggered another trend. Many Indians with international MBA degrees, who had been working abroad have started returning to India, some willingly, others out of compulsion.

For those in business (first-time entrepreneurs or the second generation within business families), there is a need to upgrade their qualifications to be competitive on a global platform – to take their businesses to the *next* level.

Money

If you had to choose only a single reason for pursuing an MBA, this might be the one that overshadows all the others. Whether money can be connected to happiness is a debate that'll go on and we won't even get into it here. However, financial freedom is also another term for peace of mind. You have current needs – a bigger house, a new car, more branded clothes, the fantastic new home theatre system you saw at the mall. And you have to plan for your future needs as well – marriage, kids' education, medical expenses and retirement. And inflation isn't helping you too much in meeting these goals. These are your productive years and you have to make the most of them in the next few years. You need to make lots of money in the next five years so that you can make sound investments that will create a regular source of additional revenue and facilitate the early retirement plans that you've been secretly intending to make for many years now.

Others

There may be other motivations as well. Some contenders might just be looking for a sabbatical, a break from their current routines, and a chance to rejuvenate themselves before they hit the corporate world again. For others, it may be a good way to meet new people and possibly bump into their life partners during the two-year stint at B-school. Some may just be too fixated on a particular school and would do anything to get it on their resumes. This explains why exorbitant short-term courses in many top B-schools play to packed houses. Senior managers and top-level executives who do not have the time but have more than enough money to compensate for it, are regulars at such courses. This is also a way some top companies reward their best performing employees in a bid to retain them.

An increasing number of MBAs have started opting for the entrepreneurial route, for the freedom, flexibility and sense of ownership it offers. Why work for someone else when you can have your own business?

WHERE'S THE NEGATIVE PUBLICITY?

Conventional wisdom says every issue has at least two sides to the story, and if that is true then the MBA story should not be any different. If there are positive things about the MBA, then shouldn't there be counterviews as well? Why is it then that the image painted by the media, when it comes to management education, is so overwhelmingly positive that you'd be ready to believe it was the best thing to hit the planet after sliced bread?

Three letters that usually go hand-in-glove with your friendly neighbourhood MBA may help partially clarify our queries: E-G-O. Every MBA course worth its salt ensures the candidates it admits into its fold traverse through a tough rocky journey right from the time they think about applying. Those who brave the barrage of information from the official websites, the Internet, current students, alumni and various publications, have already gone through a lot of bother. The actual programme is also far from the cakewalk many imagine it to be, considering they have done exceedingly well in their graduation degrees. Add to this the anguish of job hunting and most MBAs are totally drained at the end of the experience. After this ordeal, if an MBA was to tell you it wasn't worth it and that she was a fool of the highest order to have embarked on this journey, she would become the laughing stock of the entire professional community that she has been a part of and intends to be for the rest of her working life. Bloated egos of fresh management graduates would never let them accept anything but success. It's all about respect, right?

What about the other characters in the play – schools, professors, coaching institutions, rankings and headhunters? Why are they tight-lipped about it? Let's face it. For them, this is their bread and butter. And with the competition getting worse with every passing year, the only way they can sustain and grow their profits is by seeing the demand grow. More students mean more business for everyone in the MBA supply chain. No one wants to risk a domino effect here.

Just for the heck of it, imagine what would happen if 20 per cent (an extremely conservative estimate, I'm assuming) of the graduating batch decided to voice their real (and over-dramatized) opinions and said, 'This whole experience sucked. The selection process made no sense. The scholarship decisions were flawed. Except for a few common-sense concepts packaged in exotic phrases, there was hardly any real learning. The internship was a waste of time. It was humiliating and frustrating to go through the job search all over again. If I had the option of rolling back time, I'd decide never to come close to a business school again… unless I was sitting in a bulldozer.'

Exaggerated response, I agree. But if this were to happen, the word-of-mouth publicity, blogs and chat forums are powerful enough to ensure that this unauthenticated, uncensored and probably unjustified opinion reaches a big number of future candidates, who'll start getting second thoughts about their decisions to pursue an MBA. Spending on coaching classes, essay editing services, mock interviews will decrease. Advertising revenues for schools will go down.

Don't worry, it was just a bad dream (for those who have a share in the MBA pie). None of this is going to happen anytime in the near future. The hype will continue to exist and so will the information asymmetry. So it becomes all the more important for you to seek genuine information and take informed decisions.

Everything that we discuss in this book hinges upon a three-step approach (speaking like an MBA already?). At any point in time during your introspection process, if you ever feel confused by the magnitude of information or by your own conflicting views, get back to this page to realign your thoughts.

1. Identify and prioritize your individual needs. Evaluate seriously if you really need an MBA or if one of the simpler alternatives would work just as well.
2. If you are absolutely convinced that an MBA is the only option, go for a *good*[1] school that maximizes your chances of achieving your goals. Strip off the hype that surrounds the process and keep your expectations realistic.
3. If you can't get into a good school, take some time off and then go back to step one. Re-explore the alternatives (some of these are covered in Chapter 11) to reach your goals. It'll be way better than accepting an offer from a mediocre B-school just for the degree.

Simple, intuitive and logical, isn't it? But you'll be surprised as to how many MBA hopefuls get dazzled just by the idea of having an MBA degree on their resume, choose wrong schools and end up frustrated after those two years. The pursuit of an MBA becomes an end in itself.

Nine 'Good' Business Schools most Indians have on Their Radar

Irrespective of your GMAT score, your post-MBA career goals and your penchant/hatred for saas-bahu serials, if you are an Indian MBA applicant, these are the places to get into. Whether you are eligible or qualified to get into them or not, you will find most of your peers talking about them before, during and after you complete your MBA course from another university. So spend a little time getting to know these top MBA programmes.

[1] 'Good' is a flexible term that you'll come across frequently in this book. It is pretty subjective and has no absolute definition. It could mean different things for different people. We'll talk about this later in Appendix D.

1. **Harvard Business School (HBS)** – A hundred years in the MBA business and the strongest brand in the market – these are two good reasons to keep the Harvard flag flying high up there.

2. **Stanford Graduate School of Business (Stanford GSB)** – Did you know it's tougher to get into Stanford than it is to get into Harvard? Reasons – a rock solid brand that's respected globally, an opportunity to interact with brilliant (and nice) classmates and get some vitamin D (and Vitamin $ in the form of venture capital funds for your new venture) in sunny Silicon Valley.

3. **Wharton School of the University of Pennsylvania (Wharton MBA)** – After IIM (Indian/IT/Male), the next most common acronym, if you can call it that, in the B-school world is H/S/W. And the 'W' in there stands for Wharton ('H' and 'S' standing for Harvard and Stanford, of course). Very 'fact-based and data-driven'. Also quite strong in finance (and entrepreneurship), if that's your cup of tea.

4. **Massachusetts Institute of Technology (MIT)** – 'Mere paas Harvard hai, Stanford hai, Wharton hai… tumhare paas kya hai…haain?' 'Bhai, mere paas, Maaaa…ssachusetts Institute of Technology hai, bhaai'. Enough said. Its MBA programme is strong in most speciality rankings, including Supply Chain/ Logistics, Production/Operations, Entrepreneurship and Information Systems.

5. **London Business School (LBS)** – The strongest non-American MBA brand out there. Bang in the middle of London with easy access to all the top employers in the city. It offers a sixteen-month option if you are in a hurry to hit the job market faster.

6. **INSEAD** – The chhotu-sa town (in comparison to France) of Fontainebleau came on to the global map and junta started getting inquisitive (with questions like 'how the heck do you pronounce the name of the school and the town?') because of this one institution. With a campus in Singapore, it's spread its wings into Asia.

7. **Indian School of Business (ISB), Hyderabad** – Let's go beyond patriotic rhetoric and accept the fact that this is the best international B-school (being unapologetically judgemental here) we have back home that can compete with the international old-timers out there. It's cracked into the top rankings in a very short time and we've got high hopes for our strongest desi contender. Give it time and breathing space, though, as others in the same league have had a long run-up to reach where they are.

8. **Indian Institute of Management, Ahmedabad (IIMA)** – After proving their mettle in the traditional two-year MBA space, they've now moved into the one-year MBA domain – through their postgraduate programme for executives (PGPX) – and cracked into the *Financial Times* ranking of elite international schools. The idea – leverage a prestigious brand and some world-class resources (including some superstar professors and strong industry connections) to reinvent the management education game by customizing it for the experienced professional.

9. **National University of Singapore (NUS)** – An Asian programme that allows Indian applicants to learn management in an international setting without burning a huge hole in their pocket, at least in relative

terms. The low investment and attractive returns makes
it quite popular among Indian applicants.

Of course, these aren't the only 'good' schools. There are many
more that you can research based on your background, age, work
experience, budget, and post-MBA goals.

2   The Application Process

Three years into their corporate avatars, our bold friends Sachin and Mitu had done pretty well in their chosen careers. Sachin had started off as a team member doing hardcore technical work for the first two years. He developed software for the logistics industry. Due to his excellent performance and the rave reviews he earned from client teams, he was promoted to a team leader position ahead of time. In his last appraisal, he learnt that his second promotion was being considered. Again, ahead of schedule. All going better than planned for by our man.

But Sachin was nurturing another idea and working on it on weekends. He wanted to use his expertise in technology to launch his own 'start-up' company. A focused online portal for trading celebrity items (autographs, accessories and clothing used in movies, signed books, their doctor's prescription for depression pills, etc.)?[1] In a celebrity-obsessed nation like India, Sachin felt the idea had huge potential. But to transform it into reality, Sachin would need more than just a creative mind and inspiration. He needed to understand the nuts and bolts of running a business. In his current role within a bigger company, he only had to focus on the technical aspect. There were dedicated teams to take care of all the rest – managing resources, administration, accounting, marketing. For the new venture, technology and his

---

[1] If you ever think about starting a company with this idea, then in your business plan, do factor in the royalty you'd need to pay me. If you already have a website based on this idea, I bow to thee.

functional knowledge about portals would come in handy. But he'd be completely lost if he had to look at financing the whole thing, plan the marketing aspects, build a team, pitch the idea to venture capitalists and get a buy-in from various quarters. He felt an MBA was the best way to come up to speed on many of these areas.

Mitu had been doing some hard work as well in his software job in India. Not being part of the family business meant he had to slog it out and earn his stripes like everyone else around him. His boss was a tough taskmaster and Mitu didn't get the preferential treatment he might have got working with his dad. He had to learn the ropes just like everyone else and prove his mettle before he was given additional responsibility. He was also regularly warding off his dad's request to get back home and take on the reins of the family business. But the MBA *keeda* was still niggling him. He wanted to work abroad for a few years, pick up some *best practices* (buzzword alert) before he got back to his family business. He figured that management consulting was a brilliant way to pick up those skills. McKinsey, Bain and BCG (The Boston Consulting Group) were the favourites in this area on most top business school campuses.

Thus both Sachin and Mitu were ready to take the plunge into the MBA world.

Mitu was getting frustrated even before he had stepped into a B-school. The entire MBA application process, it seemed, was designed to discourage candidates from applying rather than attract them. Very soon Mitu realized his expenses were mounting even before the MBA programme had started. There were the payments for entrance test preparation, test fees, charges for forwarding the test scores to each school, application fees for each school, photocopying costs (can be quite a bit if you are outside India and not abusing your office equipment), telephone costs (international call costs could add up), Internet costs, courier charges. He had spent almost a whole year just on the application process.

Surprisingly, from the ever increasing numbers of candidates flocking towards the degree, the bludgeoning did not seem like a deterrent. All successful candidates, however, seemed to have mustered the courage and the persistence to swim against the current to reach the shores of their favourite schools.

Ivy League schools receive around fifteen applications[2] for each MBA seat and the competition for top seats is cut-throat. The selectivity rates and the barriers to entry have only climbed higher over the past few years. Many websites and consultants advise candidates to start at least a year before the target date for the programme of their choice. Many schools have several admission rounds, and the general belief in the industry is that your chances of being offered a seat in the earlier rounds is better than in the latter ones. The same applies to scholarships as well, as most of these are handed out in the first or second rounds.

CHOOSING A BUSINESS SCHOOL

You will hear this a zillion times from those who are familiar with the process. Ensure 'FIT' with the MBA programme. For Indian schools, this concept is almost non-existent. Just like the schools abroad, in India we do have schools that have a reputation of being good in certain disciplines. But when it comes to choosing B-schools, we hardly think about 'fitting' into a particular school. The general logic is, if the school has a very strong brand, it is good enough for me.

But international schools encourage you to evaluate a mutual fit. MBA alumni from top MBA programmes recommend the

---

[2] In contrast, in the IIMs, the selectivity rate is a mind-boggling one per cent! But it's not a fair comparison as the profile of students, the expectations of the schools and the entire application process are very different.

same thing. On many websites, blogs and discussion forums, you'll find prospective students who've not even got into business schools talking about this. Essentially what this means is whether there's mutual compatibility between you and the school. At a conceptual level, it means trying to address the following questions:

- Do I have the qualities that this school looks for in the incoming class?
- Will this school meet my objectives (in the areas of education, networking, career)?
- What can I give back to the class and the overall B-school community?

Appendix D has more queries that you can ask yourself to get an answer to the 'fit' question.

So you roll up your sleeves and start researching. You check out the websites of top B-schools and download their brochures. After a while they all start looking and sounding the same. Right?

You are not alone. Most schools look the same on paper. However, there are differences and you've got to spend time to find out what that is. For that you'd need to supplement the information you've got from the brochures, sites, etc., with other sources.

Alumni from top schools are a good source of information. You can get first-hand insights into their experiences. Chat transcripts with the admissions committee are another. Be prepared to get a whole lot of diplomatic answers, though. Discussion forums would be another stop for you. Use your discretion to weed out the paranoid, hyper-aggressive, overly-pessimistic/optimistic opinions. Remember that at the end of the day, most people who are active on these forums are just like you, finding their own way around. If you are willing to shell out some money, a good consultant might be able to accelerate the process and reduce the learning curve.

However, all this will still not guarantee that you are getting the complete picture as the degree of credibility, authenticity and neutrality can vary tremendously across all these channels. It can take weeks and months, sometimes years (try having a heart-to-heart talk with some re-applicants to see what I mean) to realize where and how that elusive quality of 'fit' fits into your story.

Ultimately, after doing a whole lot of homework, it comes back to gut-feel. But the more prepared you will be, the stronger your gut-feel will become.

Profile Evaluation

Evaluating your profile either on your own or by a professional can be a helpful step in choosing the right school. It can give you an idea of whether you are targeting schools that are too ambitious for someone with your profile or you are being too conservative. Either option isn't good.

If you have an unconventional profile, the story can be quite different.

'So you aren't an engineer? And you've never written a line of software code in your life? Your GMAT score isn't 750+? And your CV (resume, if you prefer) doesn't say IIT on it either? Are you sure you are from India?'

Don't worry. That's not how an admissions committee member will grill you if you aren't from the common Indian applicant pool. MBA admission officers screening piles of applications aren't looking only for conventional profiles. They don't want their classrooms to be filled up only by management consultants, tech whizkids and investment bankers.

They are also looking for people who've made their mark in other fields – medical, manufacturing, retail, energy, education and media. So unconventional is actually good; it helps you break away from the herd and carve out a niche for yourself. But it will only work if you can back it up with other strong credentials.

COMPONENTS OF AN **MBA** APPLICATION

For conventional two-year programmes offered by Indian schools that take in candidates with little or no experience, the selection boils down to one huge hurdle – the entrance exam. Of course there's the Group Discussion (GD) and the Personal Interview (PI) at many top schools. But it is essentially the competitive exam that it all comes down to. If you are lucky enough to break into the top percentile (99+ for the top IIMs), the rest is generally a cakewalk. Well, not exactly.[3] But compared to the international process, the weightages in Indian schools work differently. When a candidate is coming in with very little real-world experience, there's not much corporate exposure to judge her/him by. The short time span is hardly enough to cause major impact on the professional side and so bragging rights are limited. What does that leave us with? Academic performance, extra-curriculars and, of course, the big, bad entrance examination.

For international business schools, the rules of the game are different. Individual B-schools may differ in their application formats, but a large majority request the same basic set of requirements from prospective candidates – GMAT score, TOEFL score, application (essays), recommendations, interviews.

In addition, the school may ask for evidence of work experience, financial documents, resume, transcripts and any other supporting documents.

---

[3] There are many qualified and competitive candidates who crack the entrance tests but get rejected after being invited for an interview. So it's definitely not a cakewalk.

Graduate Management Admission Test (GMAT)[4]

In the Indian B-school context, if you are an MBA applicant, the CAT, the big daddy of them all, is just one of the entrance examinations to consider. But then you also have a whole big range to choose from – XAT, SNAP, NMAT, etc.

However, when you are applying to schools overseas, for better or worse, there's only one primary test required – the GMAT.

Indian candidates (typical profile: IT, Male, Engineer) applying to the top MBA programmes tend to have high GMAT scores. So you'd better have a competitive score to begin with. GMAT coaching classes in India offer a mind-boggling array of GMAT test preparation services, and free GMAT practice tests. It's big business!

Apart from the bigger cities (like Mumbai, Hyderabad, Delhi, Noida, Chennai, Pune and Kolkata), GMAT coaching classes have sprung up in smaller cities as well. Indian candidates have conventionally preferred classroom-based options. Now international companies like Manhattan GMAT, Kaplan and Knewton, which leverage technology to offer online GMAT preparation and coaching services over the Internet, are also reaching out to the Indian applicant pool.

A high GMAT score (preferably 700+ or being in the 90 percentile for Indian applicants) in the MBA application can be a crucial link between you and your dream business school. For lower-ranked schools (we are talking about the top 20-50 range), a 650+ score would be good. For those who aren't familiar with Computer Adaptive Standardized Tests, it can take a while to come to grips with it. So get familiar with the GMAT test structure. It is designed to test quantitative, verbal and analytical areas of the candidate.

[4] GMAT is a registered trademark of the Graduate Management Admission Council.

There are four basic components of the GMAT:

- Analytical Writing Assessment (AWA)
  This consists of one essay (Analysis of an Argument) to be written in 30 minutes and gets you a score of 0-6.

- Integrated Reasoning (IR)
  This section has 12 questions related to multi-source reasoning, two-part analysis, table analysis and graphics interpretation. You get 30 minutes for it and a score between 1-8.

- Quantitative section
  This has a mix of data sufficiency (where your reasoning ability is tested) and problem-solving questions (all multiple-choice) based on basic arithmetic, algebra and geometry. You get 75 minutes to crack 37 questions.

- Verbal section
  Get ready to be grilled on 'sentence correction' (testing your grammar, syntax and structuring skills), 'critical reasoning' (to ensure you have a logical and analytical brain), and 'reading comprehension' (can you read critically and eke out the gems?). Again you have 75 minutes, but this time 41 questions.

You get 3.5 hours for the exam, 4 hours if you include the optional breaks.

Your GMAT score will be a key focus area for the elite MBA programmes. Though business schools usually don't specifically list down the minimum cut-off limit for GMAT scores, generally the 80 percentile for most top schools is between 650 and 750. Apart from the overall score, the break-up of the individual components (verbal and quantitative scores) is also important. Candidates admitted to the top MBA programmes usually have a high and balanced score across each of these sections.

It is, however, just one of the components in your overall business school application. So your essays, recommendations, CV and your interview performance can play an equally important role. We'll talk about these in the subsequent sections.

The GMAT score is not a test of intelligence, and there are ways to increase your score. More on this in the Appendix.

If you have prepared well, you can increase your GMAT score dramatically by hundred points or more from where you started off. Some GMAT coaching companies offer money-back guarantees if you don't improve your score by X points. Read the fine print before signing up, though.

Test of English as a Foreign Language (TOEFL)

TOEFL[5] evaluates the candidate's comfort level with the Standard American English language. Well, there's also an alternative accepted by many business schools – IELTS, or the International English Language Testing System. But TOEFL is still the most popular. TOEFL is mainly applicable for candidates who do not speak English as their native language. Candidates are graded separately on their reading, writing, listening and speaking skills. This score is valid for two years.

Some schools might waive the requirement for English proficiency if you can demonstrate that you are comfortable with the lingua franca of the business world. If your undergraduate education transcripts state clearly that the entire curriculum was in English and if this has been the official language at work, you might be able to skip this step in your application process. So it might be worthwhile to check with each school you are applying to if it is a mandatory requirement. It could save you the

---

[5] TOEFL is the registered trademark of Educational Testing Services.

administrative hassle, especially when you are fighting against tight deadlines.

Application (Essays)

This is where you fill in personal details ranging from your blood group to your shoe size. This is also the place where you come across the most dreaded (correction, second most dreaded after the GMAT) section on 'essays'. And if you are guessing, no, these aren't the familiar ones that you did in school. MBA applications will not ask you to write ten sentences about the cow and why it is your favourite animal. Or, for that matter, the 500-word autobiography of a flowerpot. Aah, the good old school days! Business schools essays tend to be a little less interesting and a whole lot less creative. They can range from the mundane ('Tell me why you want an MBA and why do you want it now in your career?') to the exotic ('As super-MBA, if you could either press the green button to save the business world from disaster or press the red one to save 100 million poor souls from doom, what would you choose and why?').

In school, if you had a basic structure, it was easy to handle a whole lot of other topics by extending the time-tested approach. So, for instance, if your essay on the 'Cow – My favourite animal' got high marks and a standing ovation in class, the temptation to use the same with minor tweaks for the next set of essays ('My daddy', 'My best friend', 'My favourite teacher') was very high. If you faintly remember, apart from the phenomenal entertainment value, it did not do much for your grades.

Avoid the temptation to reuse material when it comes to business school essays. Though the essay topics proposed by B-schools have similar underlying themes, changing just the school name and submitting it just to save time can have disastrous effects. Each essay should ideally be customized keeping in mind the requirements of the school you are applying to.

Recommendations

Usually two professional references (one current and one recent) are expected or there can be a variation (one recent professional and one academic reference) depending on your choice of schools. These entries are expected to provide the admission committee independent opinions on your professional and academic skills. So if you truly believe your previous boss had the IQ of a squirrel and the linguistic skills of a Morse-code transmitter (or worse still, vice versa), then you are better off striking his name from your list of potential people to approach for recommendations.

Interview

This is the admission committee's way of ensuring that you are who you claim to be, that you know at least some of what you claim to know and that your articulation abilities extend beyond the Morse-code levels that you thought the boss was bestowed with. Be prepared to be grilled on all that you mentioned in your application form and more. The interview itself could be casual or extremely formal (usually the former) and cover a range of topics. The interviewer may throw in a few current affairs or business-related questions. Or they may put forth a case study for you to dissect.

Most often, an Indian MBA applicant sounds much more impressive in essays than during an interview. A few tips to prepare:

- Review your application components and know it inside out. Identify gaps where you can be grilled.
- Read specific threads (on various discussion forums) related to the school of interest.
- Review the website of the school again to refresh memories – find out what's important to them. Talk to MBA alumni from the school, if possible.

- Get a few mock interviews done by someone who understands how B-school interviews go. This will give you an idea of where you sound confident and evaluate the areas where you are likely to stumble.
- Experiment before the actual interview, not during.

Remember that an admissions interview can be very different from a regular job interview. So the last two points can be critical and will get you in the right frame of mind. All in all, realize the admission committee isn't your enemy. They want good candidates to get in too.

Scholarships

A top MBA programme would set you back by Rs 20 lakh to over 70 lakh, depending on whether you are targeting a one- or two-year programme from an elite school. Most schools will 'encourage' you to look for funding in your own country. Roughly, this translates to – 'sort out as many problems as you can before you come to our campus.' Some schools (including those that have the cautionary advice we just mentioned) are a little more considerate and will help you identify sources of funding before and during the programme.

But rather than depending on the business school, you'd be better off if you've already arranged a major chunk of the funding. There are two primary ways to do this – personal savings and MBA education loans (from Indian banks).

Then there are the extremely competitive scholarships offered by Indian trusts, companies, individuals (the respectful technical term here would be HNI – High Networth Individuals). Most of them don't cover the entire tuition. There are a few exceptions though and these are very difficult to get if you aren't a superstar. Partial scholarships for Indian candidates are also very tough to get. So if you get one of these, consider yourself very lucky.

Essentially, the bottom line is, if you aren't a strong candidate for the schools that you have on your list, a major chunk of your financing will have to come from bank loans, personal savings, campus income (internship, part-time work) and finally, scholarships.

In comparison to other disciplines, management education is looked upon as a commercial degree to earn big bucks. And maybe this is why the magnitude of funding and the number of scholarships dished out in MBA programmes are not in the same league as in other academic courses. Scholarships are available for the deserving few, and B-schools hand out their own share of scholarships, but a vast majority are sponsored by external organizations. The process for applying for scholarships, the wait and the ultimate decision-making process can be as tedious and grey as the B-school application itself.

PITFALLS OF STANDARDIZED TESTING

Standardized testing is one of the tools institutions rely upon to compare apples to apples. The format, type of questions, scoring pattern and evaluation are standardized so that the ultimate score of one candidate can be compared to another, irrespective of who took the test, when it was taken and where. Well, at least in theory.

While no one disputes the popularity and convenience of these tools, critics of the standardized testing concept point out several flaws. The test is not a level playing field. Many of these internationally recognized tests are administered in English and so non-native English speaking candidates may be at a disadvantage.

However, with training and practice, it is possible to score better. Again this puts rich kids, with resources to afford coaching classes and study material, at an advantage. In spite of knowing the underlying concepts being tested, some candidates may face test-taking stress and perform below their optimum capabilities.

These tests are predominantly objective in nature. In order to ease the scoring part, answers to the test questions are either right or wrong. The test does not question how a candidate thinks and approaches a problem. There is no way to judge how a person arrived at the answer.

This means if you had to choose one from a choice of four optional answers, you still have a pretty high chance (25 per cent) of getting it right even if you have absolutely no clue about the topic. In fact, eliminating the wrong choices to raise your hit-rate is actually a common test-taking strategy.

Standardized testing also opens up avenues for cheating. While this book was being written, a controversy related to GMAT cheating was gaining a lot of media coverage.[6] Thousands of candidates were being questioned about their tests, after using the services of a website to cheat. When the officials found out that students who had taken the GMAT test were posting the 'live' questions from the test on this website, they brought it down and sued it for copyright infringement. The GMAT uses a computer-adaptive format and a question bank of several thousand questions to simulate different tests for each candidate. However, given the scale at which candidates take the test (apart from the non-disclosure agreement that disallows prospective students from disclosing actual questions from the test), what stops a candidate from going online to any of the hundreds of MBA preparation sites to upload questions fresh from memory, to be viewed and practised by thousands of others, either knowingly or unknowingly?

[6] http://www.businessweek.com/bschools/content/jun2008/bs20080627_391632_page_2.htm

What's in It for the Schools?

Better Statistics (Higher Selectivity)

Top international schools such as Harvard/Stanford/Wharton have a filtering mechanism whereby candidates who don't think they are worthy enough for the top universities 'weed' themselves out of the race. Some who view MBA applications as a once-in-a-lifetime phenomenon go ahead and apply anyway without bothering about their chances of geting into these schools. At top Indian schools such as IIMs, there is hardly any filtering mechanism at work. The end impact is that the top schools globally get a lot lesser applications than our IIMs. So we aren't really comparing like-to-like. But anyway, the main point we want to focus on is that selectivity is still an important parameter to judge the prestige of a top MBA programme.

Check out the statistics page of any known B-school for data on the current batch. You will find similar data across most schools. This would include the class composition (male/female split, international students), test scores, age range, experience level, nationalities represented, undergraduate qualifications and pre-MBA careers. Most schools try to show a balanced class profile.

One word typically characterizes the academic and professional lives of most candidates before their MBA – homogeneity. Most MBA candidates would have probably interacted with classmates from the same nationality during their undergraduate days. In their pre-MBA careers, the story wouldn't have been very different, as most colleagues would have had similar undergraduate profiles. In other words, it would be highly unusual to find a doctor attending a mechanical engineering class. The same students, on graduation, would probably find themselves surrounded by other mechanical engineers once they join the operational division of an engineering company.

One of the unique selling propositions (USP) of an MBA programme is the diversity it offers. In the process of forming groups for a team assignment, the marketing professor from the MBA class may very well add a doctor to the group.

Now check out the placement page of various B-schools. They would list the post-MBA destinations for the previous class, their industry, their function, their average salary (please do remember to stop salivating after reading those figures) and information categorized according to many other parameters. Irrespective of your objective, you'll have an impressive chart that shows how others have managed to reach those goals after their MBA.

The bigger the applicant pool, the better are the schools' chances of ensuring that the charts on their websites and brochures continue to sparkle year after year.

Application Processing Charges

While most schools do mention average, median or 80-percentile scores for the key components, you would find very few that tell you what their minimum cut-offs are, especially when it comes to GMAT scores. Now think about how much you would shell out if you had to submit your application to any school after you have taken care of prerequisites such as entrance tests. On an average, it would be between Rs 7,000 to 12,000 per application.

Now consider how many applications each Ivy League school might be receiving from candidates who just want to brag about how their Harvard application got rejected for vague reasons. For the top schools, the selectivity is around 10–20 per cent.[7] They get too many applications every year anyway and the average statistics get better with each passing year to reflect the quality of the incoming class. Their financial coffers are not difficult

[7] http://education.yahoo.com/college/essentials/articles/biz/bschool-admissions.html

to fill considering the sky-rocketing fees they charge and their multi-million-dollar endowments.

But what about the other schools that are not as lucky? Any additional revenue stream, no matter how modest, is welcome. Often quality takes a backseat and it turns into a volume game.

Reputation

Many schools struggle to attract good candidates to their campuses and have to be content with those who have failed to get into their top choice schools. These are candidates who have decided to settle for mediocre schools rather than lose a year for a second shot at their numero uno options. For such schools, the selectivity rates deteriorate and this (as you might have guessed by now) is not exactly what schools are looking for. Instead of one in twenty candidates (for top-tier schools), you might be looking at one in two applicants striking gold at these schools. And no (I know what you are thinking), if you submit two applications to the same school, this does not increase your chances of being offered a seat. There are several schools where admission is almost guaranteed. This also means you get into class with a whole lot of other similar candidates who have been rejected by other top schools.

This is not a general rule, though. Many well-deserving and highly-capable students would have been rejected by the good schools either because of capacity constraints or for totally subjective (and debatable) reasons. The bottom line is that the industry, potential applicants and the world at large tags them as schools that aren't as credible as the ones higher up in the rankings. The stickiness of such tags makes it pretty tough for schools to shake off such labels.

Self-fulfilling Prophecy

It's an undeniable fact for B-schools. You get the best students. The students do well in the programme. The programme attracts the best employers. The students get the best jobs. The salaries offered are the best for MBA graduates. The alumni network becomes bigger, stronger and more influential. The school's endowments grow. It can invest in better infrastructure. It manages to attract the best faculty. The non-academic research papers published by these professors, and indirectly the school itself, gain further positive exposure in the media. All of this reflects favourably on B-school rankings that depend on parameters such as salary, faculty, alumni strength, entrance test scores, student selectivity and diversity. This helps the school stand out from the clutter. The brand recall value grows and overshadows the individual aspects that helped it get there. All this helps the school attract a better applicant pool and subsequently the best students from across the globe.

It's a cycle that takes several years and possibly decades to really show the results. The entire cycle can change directions and go the other way as well.

LIES, DAMNED LIES AND STATISTICS IN MBA APPLICATIONS

The admissions committee can see through any attempts by students to doctor their applications. Yet, applicants continue to figure out creative ways of pitching the same story year after year. Most schools clarify on their websites that they do not have an 'ideal candidate profile' in mind when they review applications and they just look for potential, uniqueness and sincerity in candidates. However, that does not stop candidates from presuming what this 'ideal candidate' might look like and the gaps they have to fill in their applications to resemble Mr/Ms Right as much as possible. If you thought you were the master of spin-doctoring, remember that there are a zillion others out there who think they've mastered the art as well. Here are some common clichés adopted by candidates in their applications.

1. 'Issues close to my heart include the environment, children's rights and poverty alleviation'
   Schools say they want candidates who are sensitive to social issues as well. You have reviewed alumni and current student profiles on the website and most of them do have some non-profit experience. Though you've never thought about any of these aspects before starting on the application process, and worked for an institution where profit-maximization was the only motto, you reach out to the local non-profit outfit and spend three to six months with them. And bingo, your resume appears more rounded and well-positioned now for your dream school. Or so you think.

2. 'Born to be an Entrepreneur'
   Working in a 9-to-5 job is so non-MBA-like and passé. If you aren't all set to join the regular glamour industries (read consulting and investment banking) targeted by most MBAs, you can still project yourself as a budding entrepreneur. This is one post-MBA career that never seems to go out of fashion. But you've never ever done anything entrepreneurial in your life (putting your neighbour's cat up for adoption in the local newspapers doesn't qualify here). Which means you have to go that extra distance to prepare a hypothetical business plan so you sound convincing in your essays and in the interview.

3. 'Well-balanced personality'
   No, we aren't talking about your tightrope walking and unicycle riding skills. You have to think about any remote connections you've had with the field of sports, dancing, singing, playing the piano, acting, writing, etc. Irrespective of when this connection died out, you think you can use vaguely constructed statements to highlight your fleeting association with the art. And it is perfectly reasonable to

state that your current hectic schedule does not leave you with the time or the energy to pursue anything else.

4. 'Thoroughly enjoy the *Wall Street Journal*'

   C'mon, admit it. You know what you really enjoy. The page 3 supplement with all those celebrity photos. You do pick up the WSJ occasionally as there is a free copy available in the office, but don't overdo it!

5. 'Most deserving candidate for the scholarship'

   As an Indian applying to international MBA programmes, you truly believe several things put you at a financial disadvantage – your current disposable income (post-tax, post-partying, post-shopping), the exchange rate for the currency you earn in, your post-MBA plans of working for a charity and six other reasons that cannot be openly disclosed in a book like this. But then the issue is, every Indian applicant talks about the same constraints. So why should the admissions committee be generous to you?

6. 'Top performer in academics'

   You say you've always been in the top 5 per cent of your class, without specifying if your class had ten or hundred students. You assume all schools and undergraduate institutions are at the same level when you say that. All admissions committees know about the IITs, a few might have heard about the National Institutes of Technology (NITs), formerly the Regional Engineering Colleges (RECs). But beyond that it's difficult for them to be completely conversant with all the tier-2, tier-3 and tier-104 level institutions that spring up every academic season.

7. 'Top performer in professional life'

   You proudly state that you have consistently been rated as an employee who 'exceeds expectations'. You do not, however, state that 60 per cent of your colleagues have received the same rating. You state that you were nominated as the 'cost-cutting evangelist of the month' two months back. You do not, however, state that the criterion for selection involved consuming the least cups of free coffee in the previous month.

8. 'Not in it for the money'
   Hee…hee…hee.
   'No, seriously.'

So what are the takeaways from this chapter? For one, judging managerial potential in applicants isn't easy or straightforward. There is a universally accepted system – of standardized tests, interviews, recommendations, application essays – in place and most B-schools follow it with varying degrees of conformity. But each of the components in the selection process has its limitations. Just because a candidate has cracked this application system doesn't make him a good manager. And the reverse is true as well. Fantastic managers won't necessarily make it through the gruelling application process.

The best schools look beyond the obvious to judge a candidate's potential. In your applications to such schools, every single part of your submission is carefully scrutinized by the admissions committee. Over the years, they've learned to separate the wheat from the chaff. They can judge a strong candidate despite the limitations of the individual components of the application process. Each constituent of your application works towards building that perception. Candidates must be able to show why each of their submissions is unique and worthy of consideration by the school.

The stringent application process adopted by the best schools acts as a sieve to filter out the best candidates from across the globe. Arguably, many employers place a greater emphasis on this filtering process than the other takeaways from the B-school experience. The generally accepted rule of thumb is that the harder it is to get into a school, the easier it is to land a good job – and vice versa. It's a similar story with our premium institutions. And we aren't just talking about the IITs and IIMs. The reason corporate recruiters value students with a degree from these elite Indian institutions is the same. The best brains from all over India have gone through a competitive selection process and only a small proportion has been lucky to get in. So if you've managed to compete with the thousands of other equally strong candidates and managed to bag one of those coveted admission offers from the best schools, it says something about your profile.

Culture Shock for Indian Students

Most of the Indian applicants have grown up on international channels beaming down rock music, English sitcoms and Hollywood movies. And they think they understand what to expect when they get into an international business school. But for many, the culture shock, specifically in the first few weeks, can still be difficult to manage.

The first thing that hits them is the climate. It's one thing to read about White Christmas and appreciate the pretty images of snow-covered streets while one is sitting in India. But it's a completely different feeling wading through knee-deep snow in sub-zero temperatures wondering what froze first, your fingers or your butt. That's an exaggeration, of course, but climate can be a concern if what you get isn't what you were expecting.

Intercultural interactions inside and outside the class can take on a whole new meaning as well. Though there are usually a few dominating influences (the nationalities that have the biggest chunk in the class composition pie-chart), there are several other perspectives that you will get exposed to. On every topic that is being discussed, the American view might be very different from the European view. Your classmates from China and other Asian countries might have a completely contrasting opinion.

And the *tough-to-swallow* fact is that they are *all* right from their respective perspectives.

If you are an omnivore you don't have much to worry about. But if you have strict dietary preferences, find out a way to get your square meal when you are away from India and home-cooked meal isn't readily available. Fortunately, most international cities have Indian (or 'South Asian') grocery shops that stock everything from Lijjat Papad to Vicks Vaporub.

The concept of dignity of labour can also be pretty alien for most Indian students. Their classmates from other countries may not shy away from taking up a waiter's job at the local fast-food restaurant or work as an attendant at a gas (gasoline as opposed to petrol) station to plug the financial shortfall. But Indian students get a thousand thoughts in their mind ranging from what their families back home would think to how their pampered egos would handle it.

If you go with an open mind, everything becomes a lot easier to adapt to.

3   The MBA Industry

Consider the population figures of the following countries: Vatican City (800), Greenland (57,000), Bermuda (65,000), US Virgin Islands (110,000), Barbados (256,000), Brunei (400,000), Luxembourg (491,700).[1]

Now compare this with the estimated number of MBAs graduating each year from business schools across the globe – half a million.[2] The number is greater than the combined population of about twenty-one sovereign states in a list of 221 countries. That seemingly unwarranted piece of trivia was just to put things in perspective.

HOW BIG IS IT ANYWAY?

If you thought the MBA story starts with the candidate, proceeds with the school and ends happily with employment, then you'd be surprised to read that the industry goes way beyond these three players and includes a much bigger network. And the biggest aspects this industry feeds on are greed, fear, peer pressure and marketing hype.

'Greed is good,' claimed the protagonist (played by Michael Douglas) in *Wall Street*, giving 'greed' a flavour of being a virtue rather than a vice. The 1987 movie is still very popular with MBA students and many share sentiments with the character played by Douglas. Greed as it relates not only to money, but also power.

[1] http://en.wikipedia.org/wiki/List_of_countries_by_population
[2] http://hbswk.hbs.edu/item/6053.html

The media regularly flashes reports about successful MBAs at the helm of many top firms, their compensation packages, perks of the job and lavish lifestyles.

Along with greed, there is also the fear of not giving it your best shot. The fear of not being able to meet your own expectations (and those of your family, friends, social and professional circles). And fear of the big F word – Failure.

Peer pressure also plays a big role in the whole process. Many hopefuls don't even disclose the fact that they are preparing for a B-school application. They would rather work in the guerilla mode and make a public announcement only after they hear some good news from one of the schools they have applied to. The embarrassment and awkwardness of admitting that the top schools did not feel your application was strong enough can be pretty humiliating.

Consider the GMAT, for instance. This test is taken around 290,000 times[3] annually by prospective candidates across the world. Indians make up a big chunk of the overall pie (about 10 per cent, at third position after the US and China) and that slice is growing[4] – 26,937 Indian citizens across the world took the test in 2008 and that number grew to 30,213 (including 23,000 residents) in 2012. Another important parameter, to get an idea about the growth, is the number of test scores sent by applicants from each nationality to international business schools. Note that each candidate sends multiple scores (4+ on an average). In 2010, Indian citizens sent around 1.3 lakh scores to international business schools. That's again the third largest volume after the US and China.

[3] Source: GMAC 2012 World Geographic Trend Report for GMAT Examinees.
[4] Ibid.

THE KEY STAKEHOLDERS

While the GMAT is the primary entrance examination, across the globe there are several schools that have their own proprietary entrance examinations as well. And many schools may not require any standardized examination score at all.

Coaching Classes

As the entrance test is crucial, the heavy dependence on scoring well in it puts candidates under pressure and generates business opportunities for those who can help ease that stress. Coaching classes that promise to turn your rusty brains into well-oiled supercomputers ready to take on the GMAT or any other 800-pound gorilla that stands between you and your MBA. All for a fee that makes you feel lighter in the pocket and giddy in the head.

Essay Services

If you have talked to current MBA students or alumni about their admissions process, in all likelihood, they would have mentioned about the formidable essays that form part and parcel of the application docket. The admission committee tries to judge the potential of a candidate by the way an essay is structured and presented.

Unlike standardized tests that follow an objective format, essays that an applicant has to submit are purely subjective. They are designed to probe the candidate, analyse their approach to problem-solving, ascertain their written communication and articulation skills and evaluate their convincing abilities.

A good international consultant may charge you upwards of Rs 22,000 ($500) for one essay for one school, and if you require it urgently, then there may be a 20–25 per cent (or more) premium added to the regular charges. If you are ready to spend more, there are package deals available as well.

Mock Interviews

This is the final stage of the application process. Unlike the other stages, where information flow has largely been one way, this is the first time you face an interactive assessment directly with representatives of the school. This interactive scrutiny is what makes this step unique. It is no wonder that this step could enhance your stress levels, when you realize that this final step could make or break your application.

At over Rs 9,000 ($200) an hour, international interview coaches offer to help you polish your interviewing skills, so that you appear cool and confident in your real interviews with the school and sail through the ordeal with ease. The fee charged by Indian consultants would be a notch lower.

Rankings

Monopoly isn't good for any industry. And the same applies to awards and rankings as well. Consider movies, for instance. The biggest awards, the Oscars, have plenty of company and competition for eyeballs from the Emmies, Golden Globes, MTV Movie Awards and a host of other movie-related awards. At the end of it, you struggle to decide who's the *fairest* of them all.

Why should B-school awards (or MBA rankings, if you prefer the term) be any different? And so we end up with numerous rankings – by specialization, by location/region/country, by category for full-time/part-time/executive MBAs, and those based on individual parameters (top salaries, international mix, etc.).

In most cases, you would find the usual suspects at the top. But at times, some of the B-schools you see in the top names may surprise you. Makes you wonder about the credibility of the ranking procedure.

It may not be a bad option to create your own customized ranking system. Consider the top five lists of rankings that you really believe in. Choose parameters that matter to you (say, career change, jump in salary and change of location – in that order). Assign weights to each ranking based on these parameters. And voila! You have got yourself a scientific-looking self-published ranking of your own to help you out with your decision making.

Many top schools stay away from rankings[5] or just provide limited cooperation, as they do not believe in the practice.

Placement Agents

Many MBA candidates are not lucky enough to land a full-time job offer at the end of their internships, and job hunting does become a real concern, especially towards the end of the programme. The careers' team at the B-school is one of the avenues such candidates try to tap into. Some companies that have had a long relationship with B-schools and have MBA-focused recruitment, approach the school directly.

Another avenue is placement agencies. However, they do not have the patience to customize their search for MBAs and the time to understand a fresh MBA's requirements. Their objective is to maximize their annual incomes by placing the most number of candidates. If you've already had seven years of experience in consulting before your MBA and you are looking to go back into consulting, your profile appears far more attractive to them than if you are looking for your first break into the investment banking sector. But in the former case, you would probably have many contacts in the industry from your pre-MBA days as a consultant and wouldn't probably need a placement agent.

The credibility of a placement agent could also be a source of concern here. There is big money to be made in this area as placement agencies' commissions can range from 10 to 30 per cent of your first year salary. This may differ based on factors such

[5] http://en.wikipedia.org/wiki/MBA

as industry, designation, country and demand/supply dynamics. And where there's honey there will be bees.

Just like other MBA consultants and specialists, there are hardly any educational or skill-based pre-qualifications required for a self-proclaimed placement agent to jump into the fray. The basic infrastructure required for this business is a computer, Internet connectivity and a phone. In fact, many do not even have formal offices and prefer to work from home.

Financing Institutions

It is unlikely that an MBA candidate will have pockets deep enough to pay for the entire costs of a good MBA programme. Well, assuming you aren't a consultant or banker or the scion of a business magnate you will need a student loan. Most business schools have a tie-up with one or more banks or financing agencies to provide this funding. Of course, you'll have to convince them that you have the potential to get back into the job market and start earning enough to pay back the loan principal along with the interest. Indian financing institutions have regulatory constraints. In most cases, twenty lakh rupees is the maximum they can provide for an international MBA course, but this amount is not sufficient to cover the entire tuition and the cost of living. So students are expected to make arrangements for the rest of the funds on their own.

Travel Industry

About 20-30 per cent of the MBA student population studying in the US is that of foreign candidates. This means there is a big demand for flight tickets, visas, foreign exchange, overseas insurance, accommodation, international calling cards. So much so that airlines competing for a revenue share from the ever-growing student pie even offer a 'student special' rate during the beginning of the academic year. The visa process can be complex and intimidating to international students travelling for the first time. So you have your local travel consultants offering their services to make your journey smooth and stress-free.

Let's now get back to our initial estimate of 500,000 MBAs graduating globally. On a very (very) conservative level, let us assume that an average candidate spends about ten lakh rupees on the MBA. This is an all-inclusive figure accounting for tuition fees, application charges, entrance exams, coaching, rent, travel, books and regular expenses. This may vary depending on granular-level details such as country, duration, B-school ranking and many such factors. At the risk of oversimplifying, we are still looking at an industry that's worth, at the very least, Rs 50,000 crore. The actual size of the industry, I'm sure, would be much bigger.

How to Improve Your MBA Profile for the Top B-Schools

Alright. The first myth-breaking moment. There is no 'ideal MBA applicant' (glass-shattering sound in the background). MBA admissions committees aren't looking for an 'A'-list candidate with Aamir Khan's creativity, Amitabh Bachchan's baritone, Amartya Sen's intellect and Mukesh Ambani's business sense.

But there is a set of characteristics that most admissions committees would find interesting in Indian candidates, an applicant pool that looks notoriously homogeneous. And the 'A' list that we just spoke about has some pointers to help us out. Let's go backwards with it.

Business sense: You don't need to be Ambani, but you do need to have a basic understanding of how businesses function. Your pre-MBA performance is a good way to highlight that. If you've had a strong professional background, if you've been better than your peers and if you've shouldered more responsibilities than your job description warranted – then you are doing well.

Intellect: This is the raw mental brainpower that drives most initiatives in your personal or professional lives. And if you aren't found lacking in that department it would be relatively safe for employers and admissions committees to assume that your efforts would be in the right direction and that they would benefit the organizations and institutions that you are associated with. Your academic grades and your GMAT score would tell their own story.

Communication skills: No baritone needed when you are making presentations and trying to sell a product or a service or just an idea. Ultimately it all comes down to your ability to assimilate all available data, structure your thoughts in your mind before your vocal chords expose your brilliant mind to the eager world waiting out there. For B-school applications, admissions committees will consider your essays and your interview to judge this.

Creativity: This is an area where even the best business school will not be able to help you. But it's that 1 per cent inspiration that you've got to summon up so it helps you utilize the other three faculties – namely intellect, communication skills and business sense. Aamir Khan might have come up with that *bald-attendants-in-every-theatre* marketing gimmick for Ghajini that everyone in the media went gaga over. That's the creativity part. For the remaining 99 per cent, it came down to his ability to plan, schedule, communicate and execute the plan. Use your extra-curricular activities to demonstrate aspects where you've demonstrated creativity, leadership, and anything else that makes you an interesting candidate – one that your classmates would love to hang out with after your MBA classes are over.

If you have time on your hands to sculpt your profile, try looking at the four areas above and see where you currently need some work.

More on Admission Consultants

With so much interest in *phoren* MBAs, do you think MBA admissions consulting in India has come of age? Far from it, actually. We are still a CAT-obsessed nation. We are talking about the Common Admission Test for entry into the IIMs. However, as pointed out earlier, the profile of the typical Indian MBA candidate aiming for the top Indian MBA programmes is distinct from the international MBA aspirant from India. The MBA selection process parameters considered by the top business schools abroad are also very different. Which, in turn, means the whole consulting approach needs to be customized for the international business school admissions process.

However, the bigger players with a huge footprint in the CAT market don't really get it. The cookie-cutter approach adopted for candidates with low-to-nil experience (where the emphasis is more on the standardized exams) cannot be extrapolated for international schools.

Thus don't be surprised if you come across candidates narrating unpleasant memories of how their 'consultant' knew far less than the candidate, used a template to answer questions, was at a loss for explanations/justifications when the candidates' queries went just a little beyond the norms. The essay editing was little more than polishing the language and in many cases the structure, grammar and presentation left much to be desired. The factory mentality permeates the MBA preparation industry. How else can you expand across the country rapidly and have a huge army of service delivery people (we refuse to acknowledge them as 'experts' or 'consultants')? The big draw for them is the low price they can offer. It also reflects in the compensation their consultants get. But you've heard the saying, 'If you throw peanuts, you will get…' Ahem…you know the rest.

MBA admissions consulting in India or abroad cannot be a commoditized service. Don't take these views at face value, do your own research. Talk to guys who've gone through the process with these bigger factories and fly-by-night operators. If they got into the schools of their choice, find out if it was because of or in spite of their 'consultants'.

Rather than engaging the wrong MBA consulting team, you might be better off managing the application process on your own.

It's a complex decision for most of us coming from middle-class backgrounds. For a top school, you are looking at an outflow of $100K+ (30–70 lakh rupees). And then there are the costs associated with relocation, visa… and MBA admission consultants.

And to complicate matters, consultants come in all varieties:

- The bulk deal (people willing to do unlimited schools for Rs 15,000)
- The upgraders (CAT coaching institutions wanting a piece of the growing international MBA pie)
- The part-timers (top-school graduates testing the waters, but holding on to their day-jobs while trying to figure out a business model that works)
- The serious ones (fantastic quality, great track record, but obscenely priced services out of reach for most Indian applicants)

It's a call you have to take, based on multiple parameters – the quality of people working with you on your application (and not some unknown face working behind the scene on something so critical), their credibility, the track record and, of course, the cost involved.

One big factor to keep in mind is trust. If you get the feeling that the guy or the team working with you on one of the most important decisions of your life is in it just for the money, run in the opposite direction. There has to be a genuine desire on the part of your advisor to get you into the best school.

How can you judge that? Well, for starters, check out how involved the consulting firm has been in responding to your queries (irrespective of whether this advice is free or paid).

- Are they providing superficial answers and MBA advice or do they immerse themselves into your world?
- Are they going by the book and giving your standard template answers or do they really know more than you do about the MBA industry and what admissions committees are looking for?
- Have they been successful in the real world out there (academically and professionally) or is this just bookish knowledge that they are passing on to you?
- Are their testimonials genuine and honest? Cooking up and pasting flattering feedback on websites is pretty easy.
- How many of their candidates are willing to reveal their identities without being ashamed of being associated with this team?

An MBA admission consultant can be your most important advisor, mentor and friend in this challenging journey. Spend time and effort in doing your homework and you will not regret your decision.

4 Teaching and Evaluation Techniques

Mitu finally got an offer from 'Bizcool Business School' in the US and though it wasn't in the same league as the other B-schools he had applied to, Mitu decided to go ahead and join. Bizcool was known more for the sporting accomplishments of its students than for their achievements in the corporate world. But that was okay with Mitu as he did not want to wait for another year and repeat the tedious application process.

'I could've read all this from a textbook. An MBA is meant to be a practical degree with focus on real-world hands-on experience.' Mitu thought to himself in the economics class as the professor drew the X & Y axes on the board and proceeded to draw the demand-supply curve for the umpteenth time to explain a new concept. 'Why, then, do we end up spending so much time in the class, surrounded by the same sixty students all staring at the board? Considering I could get an entire book on economics for a few hundred rupees, why am I paying Rs 5,000 an hour for this?'

B-schools use a variety of teaching methods to cover the diverse subjects on the course. Most of these are class-based techniques. Occasionally, the B-school may also take the students outside the confines of the class to give them 'real-world' perspectives of how business is conducted. Knowledge acquisition in an MBA programme is often facilitated using a combination of the following options.

LECTURES/PRESENTATIONS

How it Works

Depending on their position on the technology evolution curve, professors may walk into the classroom with a bunch of slides or a flash drive containing the MS PowerPoint presentation and flash the contents on to the big projection screen. In many cases there are no slides or presentations, just the professor waxing eloquent on the topic for the day. Professors may decide to use audio/video content as and when required to add variety to the teaching style and suit the topic being covered in that session.

Limitations of the Lecture Method

For a major part of a classroom lecture, there may be very little interaction with the class as the presentation is one-sided. Almost like reading a book. Of course, there might be questions thrown at the students to ensure they are still mentally present in the class. But the fact remains that a lecture usually takes on the characteristics of a monologue.

According to some estimates, the attention span of the average person is roughly around twenty minutes.[1] Of course, this estimate will change depending on which study you refer to. Now, if you consider that these MBA lectures usually are broken up into three-hour capsules (possibly with a fifteen-minute break in-between), it is easy to put two and two together and estimate how much of this actually registers in the minds of the sixty-odd students sitting in the class.

Grading

Many of the lecture-based subjects include marks for participation. Ten to twenty per cent of your overall grade may be based on this. The noble intention behind this practice is

[1] http://www.cs.utk.edu/~bvz/presentation.html

to encourage students to take an active interest in the topic and interact with the professors and other classmates, thereby increasing the collective learning experience. An MBA class has candidates with significant experience in various industries and disciplines. And in a marketing class on new product launches, if a student who has been a marketing manager speaks up about the personal challenges in this area, it raises the learning value tremendously.

Grading class participation, as you would imagine, is a completely subjective exercise. A handful of vociferous students are consistently more successful in gaining precious *air time* in each class with their command over language, diction and delivery, while the rest of the class waits patiently for their turn. At times you wonder if their monologues have any connection with the topic being discussed. The modest soft-spoken ones, who have actually completed all the pre-reading for the class and possibly have valid insights, are the ones who struggle for their precious two minutes per class.

Other ways of grading students include individual submissions, group presentations and written examinations.

CASE STUDIES
How it Works

Case studies are actual or fictional examples of issues faced by real organizations in different areas. For instance, a case study might focus on a marketing dilemma that an automobile company is facing while launching its latest model in the American and European markets simultaneously. Should it position the new model as a premium brand or a mass market option? How would this decision influence its pricing, advertising and distribution strategies? In contrast, another case may focus on an operational issue and involve supply chain-related details.

Limitations of the Case Study Method

All information required to analyse case studies is expected to be contained within its pages (the length may vary from two pages to over sixty). Some professors may allow students to access information sources external to the case study. This would include Internet-based research on the company, its competitors, the dynamics and trends within the industry that the company operates in and other data relevant to the case. Other professors may disallow this practice as it puts students with superior research skills and information access at an advantage when compared to the rest of the class. As the focus is more on how students analyse a given set of parameters rather than assessing research skills, this approach may make sense. Case studies tend to follow a similar pattern:

Study problem → Gather related data → Analyse information → Propose solution(s).

However, this is hardly how the real world operates. In many real-life situations, the problem isn't usually pre-defined. In fact, whether there really is any problem in the first place, is a matter that can be debated.

INDIVIDUAL PROJECTS

How it Works

This is where each student either chooses a topic of personal interest or is provided one by the professor, and carries out a detailed analysis of one or more key issues within that topic. The nature of individual projects can vary considerably, from being theoretical and research-oriented to being highly hands-on and practical.

As an example, an individual project in marketing may include a study of consumer behaviour while buying a product or a service. The exercise may entail actually reaching out to the target consumers and conducting a survey. The results of the survey are then analysed by the student to discover trends and patterns within the responses.

In the same area, another student may decide to study historical data from Internet-based information on product sales, growth trends and pricing strategies of existing products and then extrapolate these findings to any new product with similar characteristics.

The evaluation of such an individual project is based on the issues identified, the approach adopted for the study, the credibility of data gathered, the depth of analysis, evidence provided to support the hypotheses and the structure of the final report.

Limitations of the Individual Project Approach

In some schools, the individual project is provided as an alternative to an internship. For a majority, this is part of the numerous other assignments they are saddled with. This means the student may not be in a position to devote the time and energy to do justice to the topic, in spite of their best intentions. In order to meet the tight deadlines, the scope often gets sacrificed, the quality gets compromised and it just ends up as another tick mark on the list.

GROUP ASSIGNMENTS

How it Works

'In the corporate world, you will end up working with teams,' they tell you. 'So it is important that we add the element of team play in the MBA course as well.' Sounds logical, you say. Before you know it you find yourself in a team of five persons from diverse educational and professional backgrounds. As a team you are expected to work on the assignment and submit a common paper or make a common presentation.

Limitations of Group Assignments

The best thing about teamwork is you have others to share the workload. But if you think this distribution of work happens equally then you are wrong. You may end up thinking this is the worst possible combination of workers and freeloaders you've ever seen in a team setting.

GUEST LECTURES

How it Works

A famous business leader has launched, run and sold several businesses to earn the title of 'The Serial Entrepreneur.' And your professor thinks you'd learn a lot by listening to him talk about his own experiences. How did he get started? How did he come up with the idea of cars-running-on-water? Who gave him the initial money to get his concept off the ground? What hurdles did he face while chasing his dream? You think it is an exciting opportunity to see and hear one of you childhood idols speak on a topic of interest for you.

Limitations of Guest Lectures

Generally, guest lectures are scheduled for an hour or two. This is then followed by a reception to allow students to interact with the guest and ask questions that s/he may not have covered during the lecture.

You can imagine how much content can get crammed into this time. It is just plain impractical to do complete justice to any topic in that time. So the guest ends up taking a very small niche topic to focus on or rattles away at breakneck speed to gain as much ground as possible in a very short time frame. Both alternatives are less than perfect, as you'd agree. There may be the rare case of a student who draws major inspiration from this talk and goes on to achieve something substantial based on a key learning from this lecture. For the majority of the class, apart from the thrill of hearing a celebrity speak, there is little value-addition.

INDUSTRY TOURS

How it Works

You have stared at the classroom walls for so long now that you can point at the exact location of each crack and crevice blindfolded. It is high time you took the learning outside the confines of the classroom. The professor has good relations with a shoe-manufacturing company and arranges for a factory tour, so you can see for yourself how shoes are made.

Limitations of Industry Tours

Factories can be very complex and if you talk to a few of the workers on the shop-floor, they'd tell you they've been working there for several years and are still unsure of how the entire process works. Of course, they might have been exposed only to a small part of the entire process and may have never cracked the GMAT. The bottom line is that these tours can at best act as a tool for creating awareness and adding a dose of reality to the learning process.

Your profile is unique. So are your needs and your expectations from the MBA experience. So where does the MBA stand, as far as knowledge transfer is concerned? B-school education, to a large extent, depends on providing theoretical grounding across disciplines. Your exposure to your teachers will be limited mostly to classroom interactions and possibly a few extra-curricular activities outside the classroom. Of course, some faculty members may be more approachable than others.

Good schools attract good professors with the skills and the inclination to go beyond bookish knowledge. They can inspire and motivate MBA students to start looking at business from new perspectives. Mediocre schools may not be able to attract the best teachers and this will, in turn, adversely impact the level of education imparted in these institutions.

5 Saved by the Bell (Inside the Class)

You've struggled with the decision (to go in for an MBA or not), convinced (brainwashed?) yourself into seeing value in it, endured the tedious application process, swum through the tons of paperwork, stopped bothering about the huge debt that will be staring you in the face, bid goodbye to your near and dear ones, sold off your old car, and finally found your way into the classroom.

It's been one hell of a ride, you think, hoping it would be smooth sailing from this point onwards. And then, within the first week, it's time for a reality check. As if the pre-reading list of books that you hauled all the way from home wasn't enough, you get a whole lot of new material dumped on you right in the first week. More books, photocopies, case studies, specially coloured sheets that look like questionnaires, feedback sheets. This is the material that you'd have to digest over the next couple of weeks (no, not the entire year as you probably assumed after looking at the pile!).

CORE SUBJECTS – HOW CORE ARE THEY ANYWAY?

Many schools have a compulsory set of subjects that are categorized as core subjects. These are considered to be the building blocks for any MBA and are essential for all candidates to master before moving on. These would usually include some or all of the following:

Accounting

What you'll hear in class: Financial reporting, structure of financial statements (balance sheet, income statement/profit and loss accounts), common terms associated with these statements (sales, costs, earnings, depreciation/amortization, taxes, profit, etc.), analysing financial performance of companies, financial ratio analysis.

What it translates to: How much money does a company make? How much money has it borrowed from others? How is a company's performance reported and evaluated (for a single year and across years)? How can a company be compared to its competitors?

Marketing

What you'll hear in class: Principles of marketing, segmentation, target markets, marketing tools and frameworks (4P framework – product, price, placement, promotion), advertising, market research (primary and secondary research techniques), quantitative/qualitative analysis, Internet marketing.

What it translates to: How do we sell this product or service? Who do we sell it to? What will make it more attractive to customers? How do we price it?

Finance

What you'll hear in class: Capital investments, raising capital, credit analysis, hedging risks, mergers and acquisition, financial modelling, company valuation techniques (discounted cash flows, comparable company multiples).

What it translates to: Where do we get money from to support our expansion plans? Do we build a new facility or do we buy it? How long will it take us to get our money back from our investments? What do we do with our extra money?

Human Resources/Organizational Behaviour

What you'll hear in class: Managing employees/groups/teams, identifying organizational issues, conflict management, role of the manager, structuring/managing/executing organizational change, monitoring progress and managing resistance.

What it translates to: What is the best organization structure for our company (flat or multilayered)? How do we motivate our employees? How do we keep pace with the changing times? Who will help us achieve these changes?

Economics

What you'll hear in class: Concepts of macroeconomics and microeconomics, demand/supply relationships, consumer behaviour, price elasticity, measuring national income, economic statistics, public policies, inflation, employment, international trade, game theory and levers for regulating a nation's economy.

What it translates to: What drives the economy at a high level and at a more granular level? What levers does the government have to control the direction in which the economy is headed? What impacts demand and supply in an economy?

Risk Management

What you'll hear in class: Various types of risks, sovereign risks, foreign exchange risks, interest rate risks, commodity risks, tools for hedging risks, plain vanilla derivatives (forwards), exotic derivatives (options).

What it translates to: Where can we lose money for no fault of ours? What can we do to avoid financial loss? Which is the best way to protect against such potential loss?

Corporate Governance/Ethics

What you'll hear in class: Role of board, transparency, code of conduct, avoiding conflicts of interest, selection/evaluation/compensation for CEO and senior executives, ensuring accountability, regulatory disclosures, checks and controls within the system.

What it translates to: How can the company protect itself from individuals who are hell bent on messing up its reputation for selfish gains? Who plays the role of the big brother and keep an eye on unusually suspicious activity?

Information Technology (IT)

What you'll hear in class: Role of IT in businesses, management information systems (MIS), enterprise resource planning (ERP) systems, basic IT architecture, role of chief information officer (CIO), electronic commerce, disruptive technologies, technologies to provide competitive advantage, leveraging the Internet to conduct business, decision support systems, data warehousing.

What it translates to: How can the company use computers to improve business? Can the Internet be used to speed up things? Can computers go beyond data storage and processing?

Operations Management

What you'll hear in class: Supply chains, operations research, resource optimization, capacity planning and analysis, inventory management, process improvement, operational strategy, manufacturing techniques (just-in-time manufacturing), quality control (Six Sigma), work scheduling, identifying bottlenecks in the process.

What it translates to: How can we improve our product or service delivery process? Is the current process efficient enough or are there areas for improvement? How do we track, measure and ensure quality in the entire process?

Statistics

What you'll hear in class: Tools and frameworks to tackle mathematical and statistical problems in business, quantitative techniques, linear equations, linear programming, basics of calculus, data analysis, usage of spreadsheets and statistical packages to model and simulate business situations, decision-making systems, statistical inference, standard deviation.

What it translates to: Can we use MS Excel and other software packages to solve numerical problems? Can we simulate real-life situations using these tools? How do we arrive at conclusions based on the output?

Strategy

What you'll hear in class: Elements from the other core subjects, corporate development, portfolio approach, tools for portfolio management, strategy frameworks (Porter's 5-Forces, SWOT analysis), cost leadership vs differentiation, strategic alliances.

What it translates to: Is our current situation good, bad or pathetic? What are our competitors doing? How can we improve? Does it make sense to continue operating in this industry? Should we buy other companies or just partner with them?

The Utility of Electives

How many times have you seen someone walking into a pizza shop and saying – *'I'll just have the thick-crust pizza base. No cheese and absolutely no toppings, please.'* Well, maybe a few times. But for a majority of pizza lovers, toppings are what make the pizza special. They add colour, flavour and variety to what might otherwise have been a bland, unexciting product.

Specialization vs Generalization

An MBA was once considered to be a generalist degree that provided students with an exposure to all subjects relevant to the business world. However, electives have changed the generic face of the MBA and allowed students to specialize in areas of their choice. So you now have a mind-boggling array of choices for specializations. Some of the top schools offer more than 100 electives and there are actually those that touch 200. Who draws the line between flexibility and excess?

In order to be certified as a project management expert, a leading certification course expects candidates with a bachelors degree to have at least 4,500 hours of hardcore experience in project management. In contrast, MBA programmes claim to offer you the specialist tag after twelve to twenty-four hours of an elective. I'm guessing recruiters, many of whom have gone through the MBA drill, are already aware of what MBA specialization really means.

For specialization, to begin with, you have the advanced versions of the core subjects, that is, finance, economics, marketing, strategy. You can also choose a specific industry such as healthcare, real estate, agribusiness, energy, retail, information technology, investment banking, education, not-for-profit enterprise, entrepreneurship.

Star Professors

Each school worth its salt has at least a few star professors who succeed in getting their classrooms filled up on personal brand power. These are the acclaimed icons with published books on 'ground-breaking' concepts. Some might label these as common sense packaged in 2 × 2 matrices, but that will not make a dent on their book sales or their speaking assignments or the consulting fees that they charge to clients looking for personalized advice.

Flavour of the Year

During the dotcom days (before the bubble burst), there was a huge demand for MBA electives that had anything remotely to do with technology and the Internet. Entrepreneurship classes would spill over with students, with several people actually standing or sitting outside the smaller classes that hosted these electives. There was no dearth of wannabe entrepreneurs lurking in the portals of B-schools carrying a business plan in their pockets and a thirty-second elevator pitch just in case they bumped into a venture capitalist. They all had dreams of launching their own technology start-ups and striking gold in the next few years.

When the dotcom dream soured, the flavour-of-the-year changed. Private equity and venture capital became the new sought-after electives for hyper-enthusiastic MBAs. (Read more about this in the chapter on careers.)

A good strategy to choose electives would probably include staying away from those that are exceedingly oversubscribed. It might be an indication of where the next bubble is going to form.

Whatever the underlying reason is, specialization looks cool on the resume and (allegedly) enhances the market value of the candidate. It helps him or her break away from the general MBA market.

PERFORMANCE EVALUATION

We have already talked about class participation. Let us consider the other primary ways in which knowledge transfer is tested.

Individual submissions

Students are expected to work on a case study on any specific topic, carry out their own analysis, work on a report on their own and submit it. It is easier said than done. For some non-English speakers, reading through volumes of cases, books and printouts written in cryptic business language and coming out with equally formal sounding submissions can be a big challenge.

Most concepts and ideas covered in B-schools have been recycled for years. If you think your response to common business problems is absolutely original, innovative and never-seen-before, then you might be the next management guru on the horizon!

This brings up the other sinister side of the coin. What you will come up with in your individual submission may have already been discussed, published and beaten to death many times over by other researchers and students. You would have agreed to abide by the non-plagiarism policy of the school. Will you be able to resist the temptation to give into time pressures and choose the easy way out by downloading readymade reports from the Internet or utilizing 'overnight report writing services' offered across the continents? Tricky and sensitive topic.

Group Presentations

On an average, three to five (and sometimes more) students are tested based on a joint presentation. Just as in the previous case of individual assignments, a management- or business-related issue is handed over to the group to mull over. The group is expected to prepare a short (usually 15-minute) presentation to propose one or more solutions to tackle it. You'd think businesses work in teams, so this is a good way to learn. However, the difference here is that in the corporate world hierarchies are pre-defined and there is no confusion as to who calls the shots. Unfortunately, in B-school groups, every new team goes through the process of power struggle. The basic rule you learn in class is 'Teams need leaders.' And I wouldn't disagree with that, since you'd need someone to set the direction, manage conflicts, delegate work and act as the overall coordinator for the group. If you have a single dominant personality in the team, the road is a little less rocky for the team, as there is no conflict for the leader's role. It's highly likely that this one person will steamroll the others and end up wearing the crown. In case there is more than one such specimen in the team, there is bound to be trouble. You may decide to go without a leader and end up in a more chaotic situation.

All team members will not contribute equally. The more proactive and enthusiastic ones may demand a bigger piece of the cake. Others may hate the role that has been passed on to them. After a lot of heated discussions, let's say you have a fantastic presentation ready. Now the next important question is: who will present?

Option 1: One person presents and basks in the limelight while the others stand with arms neatly folded on one side of the class, silently cursing.

Option 2: Two or three present, while the remaining two continue to stand in the exact same position as described in Option 1.

Option 3: All five present for three minutes each (one minute per slide) and the entire presentation looks like a ballet performance, a visual spectacle.

Written Examinations

You have learnt all the formulae by rote, you can rattle off the ten exact steps (not one less, not one more) in which organizational transformation can be executed, you know how beta[1] can be leveraged and unleveraged while performing company valuations. You would be expected to spend three hours on a desk along with the rest of your classmates, cranking out handwritten answers.

So far so good, you'd say. This is how it's been for us since elementary school days. So where's the catch? The catch is that in the 'real world', apart from the notes that you'd scribble down during meetings, it is unlikely that you'd spend long hours writing analytical reports by hand. The repetitive strain injury (RSI) that you'd develop on your wrist will most probably be due to typing and not because of writing.

B-schools do provide a broad understanding of multiple areas in a short span of time. They may also expose students to career options that they might not have considered earlier. However, the time spent on each sub-topic is seldom sufficient to do complete justice to it. This isn't too different from other fields of learning. At the end of the day, the real expertise comes from being in the job.

There can be some value in knowledge sharing in a peer group and class discussions. But again, this value is limited. Success stories will frequently be hyped up and narrated in class by your classmates. Real life stories of failures, where most of the learning can be drawn from, will often get downplayed or are hardly discussed. No one wants to sound like a loser in a classroom filled with ambitious young people. It is a two-year mating game and everyone wants to put up their best show. It started with the application process and will continue till you bag a job.

---

[1] Beta: A parameter to capture volatility and statistical variance.

6 The Skills Gap

SKILLS REQUIRED FOR THE BUSINESS WORLD

Businesses are complex multidimensional entities that require a wide range of resources to function effectively. The core of any business is a set of products or services that the company provides to customers. And to deliver these products and services, it is essential to have the relevant skills and knowhow, or, in other words, an operations team.

There are a host of other functions that support this technical team in the delivery process. These teams make up the corporate departments and include accounts, human resources, finance, communications, corporate planning/development, information technology, legal, logistics and administration.

A company in the construction business, for instance, depends a lot on a strong track record of several high-quality projects that it has successfully executed to establish itself as a credible player. This is possible only if it has experienced civil engineers and architects with proven skills on its payroll. These technical teams are supported by corporate teams. The legal team would review all contracts that the company enters into, manage litigation cases and provide legal advice on new ventures. The finance team would help in raising finances for new projects, negotiating terms with banks, hedging their commodity risks by entering into forward contracts (for cement, steel), and parking excess funds in appropriate short- or long-term financial instruments.

SKILLS THEY ATTEMPT TO TEACH

MBAs enter the business world in operational as well as corporate roles. Irrespective of that, there are certain generic skills one can expect to pick up during the MBA. The question is: Are these really as important in the current day and age? Try to answer this by reading through some of the important skills listed in the following sections.

Data Analysis/Information Processing

In the business world one can get overwhelmed with the amount of data that gets generated. Most of this information overload is actually useless detail in the big picture. This is what necessitates the need to plough through this pile and figure out what is relevant and what can be discarded. Often, there are patterns that can be derived from this data heap, which in turn can be useful in making business decisions.

Consider, for instance, the task of rating existing and potential customers within a business. For the existing ones, there would be historical data on their transactions. What products/services did we sell them? How much did they pay for it? How many times have we entered into disputes with them for payments or quality of deliverables? How much time/effort have we spent in fire-fighting for this customer? Do they pay us on time?

For potential customers, there is again a similar set of queries. How big are their operations? How many years have they been in existence? Are there litigations and cases pending against them? What is their overall reputation in the market? Should we do business with them? What should our terms and conditions be? Can we approach contacts within the industry to find out more about them?

Valid questions, we would all agree. And if the business operates in an area that has several thousand customers, the data generated can be humongous. In the life cycle of this data, there are three distinct phases – creating/updating the data, processing and deletion/archives. Tools such as Customer Relationship Management (CRM) software are used across nearly all organizations of credible size to manage these phases. Creating new customer profiles involves gathering all relevant data for each customer and feeding it into the CRM package. This is basically a data entry role and staffing an MBA for this is overkill. Old records are archived and moved out of the system for traceability and auditing reasons instead of being erased completely.

The data processing part can be the most complex in the life cycle. However, the CRM makes this data-crunching task easier by using pre-built and pre-packaged features within the software. For managerial consumption, in most cases, this processed output is more useful than the actual data. Apart from the manual data entry, most other activities are automated. In specific areas where software tools are not available, the business can always approach consultants to create software models for them. So unless you plan to be on the other side and actually design and build such tools, you can be assured that the tedious part of data-crunching can be managed with off-the-shelf tools.

Multitasking

In B-schools, you will constantly be juggling multiple lectures, assignments, presentations, social/career/academic events. And over a period of time, you are expected to be able to manage all this without pulling your hair out in frustration. Often you would be part of multiple study groups and required to commit time for team meetings. Even after a perfect schedule has been drawn on painstakingly, there is always the chance that one of the events gets re-scheduled and you are back to square one. It may not even be possible to get involved in all activities due to overlapping schedules and time constraints. In these situations, you would have to decide which of the mutually exclusive events are higher in priority. And if you have good time management skills, this is not a big challenge.

In the corporate environment, the story is similar. Unless you are part of a highly specialized field where work schedules and processes are extremely well-defined (the assembly line in a manufacturing company, for instance), very rarely will you find that you are working on just one task. And the situation just gets worse as you rise within the organization. But the same rule applies. If you have the knack for time management, you will manage anyway, whether it is in an academic setting or in a corporate environment. Multitasking is something that cannot be taught formally in a classroom.

Theoretical Foundation

The accounting professional may be keen to understand the operational aspects of the company, the drivers used by the marketing guys to position the company's products, the strategy that senior management has in mind to help expand the business in Latin America, where the company's footprint is still small. The accountant knows that he may not actually shift into any of these other areas, but the theoretical grounding will help him gain overall clarity about areas within the company that he earlier treated as blackboxes without bothering to find out what goes on inside. But does this justify two full years in a classroom? Our man could probably have fixed informal lunch sessions with his colleagues from various departments to get an overview about their roles and figured out how it all ties in with his work. In an interactive one-on-one meeting, his queries can also be very specific. As the primary context and business setting are familiar to both parties, the responses in turn would be more meaningful and the data assimilation process more effective.

Communication Skills

A dreaded part of the MBA class experience is 'cold calling'. During case study discussions or regular lectures, the professor may randomly call out student names and ask them to explain their views on the topic of the day. Students are expected to come prepared with their pre-readings for the day and are expected to have analysed specific topics, concepts or business problems. For every point that gets expressed, there may be umpteen counter-arguments from other classmates, considering the diversity within the class. Getting your points across solidly requires a combination of clarity of thought, confidence, vocabulary and lucid speech delivery.

Similar attributes are required during individual and group presentations in class. Additionally, all group activities require people skills in order to zero in on a common set of objectives and lead the entire group towards that goal.

There's no denying that these skills are required in the business world as well. But the question is how much progress would someone with weak communication skills make in a classroom setting. Are cold calls, study groups and presentations good enough to help you brush up the entire gamut of your communication skills?

Simulations/Modelling Situations

Decision making in real life can be pretty complex. And so academicians have come up with the concept of models and simulations. This involves creating a smaller, and at times oversimplified, 'model' of the real-world situation. Software tools such as spreadsheet applications are used to identify levers that impact the model.

If this is sounding too theoretical, let us take a simple example. Say, we make an investment in a mutual fund that has historically provided 15 per cent returns per year on an average. You are considering investing Rs 1,000 in it for five years and would like to know how much you would get back at the end of the investment period in the best- and worst-case scenarios. This is a classic case of scenario modelling. In the spreadsheet, you would identify basic input parameters (for example, investment amount, period, best-case rate of return) and the output parameters (for example, amount after five years for various scenarios). You would then establish a link between the input and output parameters using appropriate formulae. And voila, your model is ready. All you have to do now is enter values for various input parameters and obtain results.

But it's not as simple as it sounds. Models and simulations can get really complex as the accuracy and the credibility of the results are driven mainly by assumptions and inputs that go into these models. For instance, in our previous example, the designer may have two input values, one for best-case returns and one for worst-case returns. Now the user may enter values for both (say, 50 per cent and 10 per cent, respectively) and the model will provide some results. What's the guarantee that the input values that go into the model reflect reality? How would you ensure that your estimates and assumptions are not too ambitious or too conservative? Many would actually drill in further details in order to capture underlying assumptions for each input parameter and try to make the model more accurate. This could mean defining complex relationships between the best/worst case returns to more granular parameters (industry growth, interest rates and global economy factors) that influence them.

We are not trying to say models aren't useful. They are, to an extent, and firms around the world have spent a lot of effort, time and money in building and maintaining their own repository of models. Some of these are more complex (and less useful) than others. Some are built in-house by corporate personnel for routine activities like budgeting and forecasting. Some are crafted by external consultants for special situations. However, the common attribute that spans across all such models is that they are driven by the Garbage-In-Garbage-Out (GIGO) concept. In other words, if you feed in trash, all you get from the model is trash, irrespective of how sophisticated the model may be.

Most good business managers realize this limitation and use models to whet their own business judgement while making critical decisions. Models and simulations are not an alternative to experience and basic common sense. How many managers and leaders that you read about in the media are applauded for their fantastic financial modelling skills?

Planning

Here we are not referring to technical planning of the kind required in operational research. We are referring to *general planning* (for lack of a better term). Defining the objective, evaluating various options and initiatives to accomplish it, estimating resources (time, money, people and effort) required for execution, identifying dependencies and finding workarounds are some of the sub-activities that would come under the general purview of planning. In B-school, planning is a continuous process as class schedules, assignment deadlines, group activities, outings, cultural events, all keep on piling non-stop. MBAs have to learn how to cope up with this workload and stay on top of it all or risk getting buried in the avalanche. Prioritization is one of the most important skills in planning. The 80:20 rule – that a small minority (20 per cent is only an indicative figure) of factors can have a big influence on the overall picture – applies to many situations and can be used as a lethal weapon in the prioritization process. For instance, twenty (of the hundred) suppliers of an electrical product may have an 80 per cent share of the market. Similarly, if you have ten open tasks to take care of, two of them may be the most critical.

But unlike the theoretical subjects, MBAs are expected to pick up this skill 'on the job'. It is assumed that the MBA student is well aware of all major milestones over the coming day, week, month, semester or even beyond, and will plan accordingly.

WHAT THEY CAN NEVER TEACH YOU AT B-SCHOOL

Leadership

In the class, you will come across a whole range of personalities – the silent, the arrogant, the super-intelligent, the vociferous, the subdued, and the life-of-the-party types. For many group activities, the Type A personalities invariably end up dominating the show and assuming leadership roles.[1] But does that automatically mean they are good leaders? We can't accept or dispute that without getting into the details on a case-by-case basis. Leadership can be considered as an amalgamation of many traits that are listed in this section. Consider each of them and evaluate for yourself if it is a quality that you already possess or if it is something you need to cultivate. If it is the former then the answer is clear. If it is the latter, then ask yourself if and how a business school degree can impart it to you.

Common Sense

A doctor comes for a routine check-up during visiting hours, while the patient's family is still around. After testing the patient's pulse, the doctor announces, 'I'm sorry, but he's dead.' As the family members start crying, the patient gets up and says, 'Guys! I'm still alive.' In response, one family member retorts, 'Shut up! Do you think you know more than the doctor?'

It's an old joke that may not evoke any laughter, but it highlights a relevant point – our tendency to get so enamoured

---

[1] Friedman, M. & Rosenman, R. H., *Type A Behavior and Your Heart*, (New York: Knopf, 1974).

by data and technical details that we overlook the obvious. We think specialists have all the answers, just because they have been in the business for years. Business schools are good at providing fancy tools and techniques to solve problems. At the end of the MBA programme, for every strategic or technical problem, you would be able to rattle off various frameworks and methodologies that can be used. With so many tools under your belt, you will find it hard to acknowledge the fact that there was a world in existence before MBA programmes were started, a world with problems, and the horrifying thought that people would still tackle these problems without an MBA degree.

Control

This could mean many things in different contexts. In management lingo, this is closely linked to planning and refers to process control. It involves monitoring the process, ensuring that events are happening as planned and taking corrective action if there is any risk of derailing. But here we are not talking about operational or organizational control, but about the psychological aspects of control. In an organizational setting, too much of control can get you labelled as a control freak. And the other extreme can be equally damaging. A total lack of control can cause chaotic situations that may be difficult to reel in. Corrective action ends up utilizing far more resources than prevention and the proverbial stitch in time. A basic rule of thumb says too much flexibility is as bad as micro-management. But you will not come across any computer-generated simulation that will tell you how much control is good or bad.

Control could also be viewed in terms of emotions, especially negative ones such as anger and greed. Many of our personality traits are inherited or drilled into our psyche after years of conditioning. A shy MBA cannot transform into an extrovert at the end of the programme. An impatient student will not automatically learn the virtues of being patient. We talked about Type-A personalities. Most of them may be aware about the pitfalls of continuing to live a stressed lifestyle. However, many of their pre-wired features are so strongly ingrained in them that pure logic and reasoning aren't sufficient to turn them around.

Practicality

Given unlimited resources and time, anything would seem possible. And in a classroom environment where there is little at stake, it isn't too difficult to get carried away by hypothetical discussions and overestimate the efficacies of your newly gained skills. It is one thing to be able to provide convincing arguments and propose creative solutions to case studies. The only guys to resist and challenge your theories and solutions are your classmates and your professor. There are no legal implications, no employees demonstrating on the streets, and no country-specific regulatory constraints. Irrespective of how good or bad your recommendations are, there is no risk of losing money, competing firms gaining a foothold in your market, stock price plunging to never-before-seen depths, attrition rates shooting through the roof. In a case study, without batting an eyelid, you can coolly recommend laying off 2,000 employees to meet the cost-cutting goals of a company and still be able to go home and sleep peacefully without having to worry about the repercussions.

Creativity/Innovation

Take any successful company and try to list down the top five things that make it special. And innovation will likely be one of these attributes. Innovation not just as it applies to high-technology products. Innovation in the company's regular manufacturing process, quality assurance, customer interactions, human resource policies, incentive schemes, career growth opportunities. The rest of the industry calls these as best practices. For instance, the Toyota way of working has been documented, studied and copied by many other firms. In fact, it is highly likely that one or more of your case studies will focus around Toyota's production system. But in spite of all this research by academicians and practitioners, other companies have found it difficult to match Toyota in the manufacturing area. This just means that the secret ingredient of innovation cannot be packaged in capsule format and gulped down in classroom sessions.

Judgement

Private equity (PE) funds raise huge amounts of money so that they can invest in companies that have a substantial growth potential. PE funds are managed by very small teams and are extremely selective in their hiring. Check out the online profiles of some of these funds. Focus on their qualifications. Almost all top-tier PE funds have super-achieving MBAs on their rolls. Given the size of their investment funds and the number of companies across the globe, you would assume there is no paucity of right opportunities to invest. But despite the background work of screening companies and the number-crunching, most investments do not yield the returns that were initially estimated. The best case/worst case modelling that we talked about earlier gets pretty complex here. But none of the MBA techniques can guarantee that the fund will make a killing on 100 per cent of its investments. At the end of the day, it is a judgement call made by the managing partners of the fund.

Foresight

Consider the case of top-tier investment banks. They recruit some of the best minds in the world at obscene salaries. They have access to the best databases with cutting-edge information, the best analytical tools, the best processes and the best contacts in the business. Almost all of these banks have sophisticated risk-management systems and trained personnel to use them. Management information systems implemented by various departments carry out in-depth analysis and churn out comprehensive reports that can be used by senior management teams to evaluate impact and take corrective actions if required. And yet, most of them had no inkling about the sub-prime crisis that hit them in 2008. Many had to write off multibillion dollars of bad debts. Out of the thousands of super-bright MBAs that these investment banks have on their payrolls, even if a handful had raised the alarm bells in advance and convinced their managements to sit up and take notice, could the magnitude of damage have been controlled? Or were the short-term rewards so overwhelmingly attractive that the few alarm bells that did get raised met with a swift painless death? Well, your guess is as good as mine.

Decision Making

We talked about judgement earlier. Decision making depends on it and both go hand in hand. Ever looked out of the window at clear skies and decided that you'd still carry an umbrella? That would be decision making at its simplest. In your mind, you subconsciously digested all the relevant information and came up with a probable outcome, that is, the possibility of rain in the next one hour appears to be low. But considering that you were in the middle of the rainy season, you discarded all that subconscious processing and insisted on carrying an umbrella. This has a lot to do with gut-feel.

Whether you are an employee working in a big corporate environment or an entrepreneur running your own show, you will come across situations where you have to make decisions. In early years of the career, there is little experience to fall back on and most decision making follows a more objective and theoretical route. Which is why, the criticality of decisions mirrors the organizational hierarchy. The senior managers make the more critical decisions. The theory, concepts and tools that the top manager works with are not too different from those used by the freshly minted MBA. So why is there this disparity? The answer lies in the grey hair, not just grey matter.

Interpersonal Skills/Relationship Management

Many important business deals are made in informal settings, across coffee tables, on golf courses, during unplanned lunches. Products and services are rapidly getting commoditized across industries.

In the wealth management industry, a commonly used term that triggers salivating mechanisms within the wealth management community is High Net Worth Individuals (HNWI or HNI). These are ultra-rich customers who apparently own private money-minting factories, but have no inkling of what they can do with their money. Or they may just not have the aptitude or the time to do it themselves. Wealth managers help them take their investment decisions. As wealth managers move from one financial institution to another, they take with them several loyal HNIs. Business development, marketing, sales are all examples of external customer-facing functions that depend heavily on relationships to keep the company in business.

Even if you are not in an external interfacing role, interpersonal skills are still hugely relevant. Attrition is a big problem for many organizations. During exit interviews, apart from expected reasons such as money and better prospects, many employees cite their difficult bosses as a key reason for moving on. This does not come as a surprise as corporate folks spend more time with their bosses and colleagues than with their spouses, family and friends.

Real-Life Experience

The school of hard knocks, as they call it. Case studies in B-schools can only provide snippets from a CEO's diary. Though they are often based on real cases and data, we have to consider the constraints of these. How much detail can one fill into thirty-odd pages of text and graphics? All the emotions that cloud the mind, the anxiety that precedes the decision-making process, the sleepless nights weighing the pros and cons of each option, the stress of meeting expectations of stakeholders and the fear of failing. An MBA sitting in the class feels none of this.

Negotiation Skills

If I say that barring a few things such as ethics, basic values, principles (think of others that fit the bill), most things in life are negotiable, would you think I'm stretching it a little too much? Right from childhood, we try to negotiate our way into the world. For most of us, our negotiation techniques have evolved over time. And we have learnt the right way from the wrong way, by practising, by messing up one too many times. Our initial efforts may not have been super-effective. But we have learnt from our mistakes. We have observed and realized that what works for others may not work for us and that there is no right way to negotiate. You will continue to use these skills in B-school and in your new job.

In class you will hear terms such as win-win approach, mediation, arbitration and BATNA (Best Alternative to a Negotiated Agreement).

Companies often use the services of professional negotiators to resolve disputes. If issues could be resolved amicably between two parties (that employ an army of MBAs who've taken up the 'Negotiation skills' elective), there would have been no need to get a third party involved.

Emotional Intelligence

Daniel Goleman popularized this concept. But if heavy technical words scare you, we can go with the less scary equivalent – maturity – though it does not entirely capture the essence of Goleman's concept. Proponents of this theory say Emotional Intelligence Quotient (EQ) can be more important than Intelligence Quotient (IQ). The four basic capabilities involve recognizing emotions, analysing them, using them appropriately and regulating them in such a way that the end objective is attained. Many organizations incorporate psychometric tests in their recruitment process in an attempt to delve into the minds and gain a better understanding of how the individual may react in various situations and predict behaviour. Again this is one of those areas that's hard-wired into each of us. With training and practice we can try to gain awareness and control on our emotions (heard of anger management sessions?) and consequently influence our behaviour.

The primary message that this chapter tries to convey is that there are several skills that can be compensated for by managers with commonly adopted approaches such as delegation and outsourcing. However, certain skills, especially at senior levels, cannot be compromised. These are the attributes that actually separate the professionals from the masses in the business world. And many of them cannot be transferred in a classroom setting to those that lack the aptitude. Those who possess the aptitude can pick up and polish these skills over time in their regular work environment without having to sacrifice their jobs for them.

'Network, network, network!!!!' was the name (plus or minus a few exclamation marks) of a popular discussion thread on the B-school chat forum. Mitu had spent hours on this site reading about how a network is all that you really take away from B-school. And he had read this in so many places and so many times that he had almost started to believe he was paying a hundred thousand bucks for his MBA for a few hundred names in his email address book. Mitu had visited the career pages of several B-schools to see how people landed all those fantastic jobs on completion of their MBA programmes. The standard 'Sources of Jobs' pie-chart on many of these pages would invariably attribute substantial percentages to helpful alumni.

Mitu always considered that the 'Chicken Soup for the Soul' series was uplifting. But that was before he discovered the careers section on B-school websites. Mitu was ecstatic. 'Imagine the post-MBA possibilities with alumni connections like that.' Now was his chance to build his very own flesh-and-blood network of generous like-minded people.

WHAT DOES IT MEAN AND HOW DOES IT WORK?

Networking in B-school lingo refers to the links that candidates build within the student community, with professors, industry experts, alumni and the corporate world. It is considered by many as an effective tool to have, especially during the critical job-hunting phase.

Networking is facilitated through many formal and informal events that are organized by the MBA administration team, the faculty and by students themselves. The informal approach to networking may include class outings, treks and weekly get-togethers organized by student clubs or individuals who have completed their academic commitments ahead of time. This provides an opportunity for students to get introduced, to intermingle in casual settings and to get to know each other on a more personal level.

A common glue binds (and accelerates) many of these informal events – alcohol! Considering the overdependence of several candidates on this glue, the formal category of networking events – guest lectures, workshops, special interest groups – may also incorporate alcohol in some form or another.

WHY IT DOESN'T WORK FOR A MAJORITY

In theory and depending on expectation levels, also in practice, networking does have its benefits. Where it can and often does go haywire is in the execution part. And there may be several underlying reasons for this.

Class-size

The size of a regular MBA programme, with several hundred students spread across various batches, can become a constraint when it comes to knowing your batchmates. B-schools intentionally try to encourage diversity in the classroom by ensuring a good mix of people with diverse educational, professional and cultural backgrounds. However, as they say, birds of a feather flock together. Over time, groups tend to form within the class based on common interests, nationalities, etc. Nothing inherently wrong with it as this is basic human nature. But imagine what this could end up doing to their collective networking graph.

If you are from the IT industry and if you are (or have been) fortunate to be staffed on an onsite assignment abroad with other team members from your Indian office, you would find a familiar sight during lunch- or coffee-breaks or weekends. A bunch of Indian professionals (including you) huddled together at the lunch table or near the coffee vending machine, cracking desi jokes, talking about the latest Bollywood or Rajnikanth flick that you can watch over the weekend in Little India (or whatever the locality is called in that area). All this happens with your little close-knit team being totally oblivious to the stares of passers-by and colleagues, some of whom manage to give you a polite smile as they move on with life.

At B-school there's a high likelihood that the story repeats itself if you are not ready to discard the huddle phenomenon. Can't blame us, right? That's how we operate back home. That's the social fabric that bonds us and makes us comfortable when we are so far away from our *matrubhoomi*. Unfortunately, it is a clear recipe for getting cut-off from the rest of the B-school community. Sticking to your comfort zones would mean you don't venture out to explore all that an MBA has to offer.

If you've been exposed to the international educational setting at an early age (for instance, while completing your undergraduate degree abroad), chances are your idea of networking goes beyond being restricted to your *homies*. For the older, mature folks who get thrown into an international academic environment at a later stage, when they are a little more inflexible and a little less willing to put themselves in unfamiliar territory, the story tends to be a little different.

Workload

Many programmes are known for their backbreaking workload. Often, there are several events that overlap or clash with assignments, submission deadlines, exams and presentations.

During such phases, networking drops to number 53 (or somewhere close) on the priority list, the top-five being breathing, working on submissions, eating, worrying about the debt, and sleeping – though not necessarily in that order.

Attitude

Though the MBA course is considered as the flagship programme by business schools, it is just one of the many that runs in parallel. There may be several other masters- and doctorate-level courses that are managed with very little formal interaction across streams. This also means there's always competition for shared resources, such as computing facilities, library, classrooms, faculty and most importantly, career resources. Students of some executive programmes are also officially eligible to become alumni. This could give rise to an us-versus-them mentality and self-obsessed MBAs may refuse to treat specimens from lower species as being worthy of networking.

Paranoia

Alumni in companies that they've struggled to get into may perceive it as brand dilution (not to mention potential competition) to have more employees from their own schools crowding their secure and cosy corporate space. This may be rare but still something to think about. In some smaller businesses, where branding is extremely important, the reverse may actually be true. For instance, in private equity funds, it isn't uncommon to have a majority of partners and senior members from the same B-school.

STRAIN ON PERSONAL RELATIONSHIPS

'My partner will be joining me in a couple of months,' Fazulbhai, a member of Mitu's first learning team, had said when the team had their introductions. Four months into the programme, there was still no sign of Fazulbhai's partner. It was only later that he admitted, 'We've been having our issues for a while and with all these other commitments it's been tough for both of us. We've decided to part ways.'

Unlike undergraduate programmes, the average MBA student is older and a good number of candidates (over 30 per cent) are involved in serious relationships. There are quite a few who are married and have children. Many B-schools recognize this fact and have 'partner clubs' that organize events for significant others to share the MBA experience and not feel left out. But whether these events compensate for the stress and pain that precede and follow these events, is anybody's guess. For the MBA ride can be even more difficult for partners, who are expected to provide psychological and moral support and play the role of friend, philosopher and guide at the same time while the *real heroes* tackle their truckload of obligations. And this usually appears like a one-way street as the partners' aspirations and goals get pushed to the backburner. As MBA students take on 'superheroic' assignments and responsibilities inside and outside the class, there is also a nagging insecurity for partners that can span from 'I look so insignificant in comparison' to 'He seems to be spending too much time with Suzy. Is there something cooking between them?' MBA is tough on long-distance relationships. No wonder then that many refer to the MBA as 'The Divorce Degree'. On the positive side, quite a few students find their soulmates during the MBA programme.

SPECIAL INTEREST GROUPS

'Sounds fantastic,' thought Mitu when he first looked at the list of Special Interest Groups (SIGs) on the school's website. 'I'd definitely want to be part of the SIGs for management consulting, investment banking and private equity.' Now after several months of being a member of seven SIGs, he doesn't appear as impressed:

'It seems like a big farce now. Apart from the encouraging high-energy first few meetings, those who launched new SIGs or chose to lead existing ones seem to be pushing their own personal agendas. It has been a great vehicle for self-promotion for a select few. Even the guy who leads the venture capital group is struggling hard to get a foothold in the VC industry. You know what's ironic? He is one of the few who had managed to land an internship with a venture capital firm.'

An SIG is meant to be a vehicle for networking and sharing knowledge where MBA students get to meet like-minded people with common interests in an industry or topic. At the beginning of the year, a bunch of enthusiastic people get together to join (or create) an SIG linked to a particular topic. The most popular ones are invariably linked to the highest paying and the most glamorous fields. Over the last few years, management consulting, investment banking, private equity/venture capital, entrepreneurship have been hot favourites. Many perceive this as a status upgrade, as it gives them the option to be associated with areas that they may be desperate to get into and will hopefully impress potential employers when they see this on their CVs. The fact that they attended only two introductory meetings of the group may be an insignificant detail that can be conveniently skipped in the CV (for lack of space) and during interviews (for lack of time).

Over the course of the year, SIGs organize events that may be of interest to a majority of its members. This could be in the form of informal knowledge-sharing sessions where students who have already worked in certain fields share their experiences and technical aspects. The SIGs may also invite prominent industry personalities to give a talk on industry trends, their own companies, how these are structured, what they do and how they do it. There could be panel discussions where several industry names get invited.

Many of the good schools pride themselves on the strength of their alumni networks. That network does carry a lot of weight, as you'd have alumni from previous batches in senior and influential positions across geographies, industries and functions. An area where this can help is in getting your foot in the door, a critical advantage when you are looking for a job after your MBA.

There are two aspects to networking and a handshake best symbolizes the process.

You have to make the effort to reach out. No two ways about that. It helps if there's a common thread that binds the two of you together and it doesn't necessarily have to be an MBA degree. It could also be a common friend or a love for football. If the other person is receptive and considerate, he or she will offer a helping hand irrespective of your alma mater.

8 Internships

'Damn these bloody corporate processes!' Mitu was upset. He had approached over a dozen companies in the hope of landing an internship and the process was excruciatingly slow. Like the rest of his class, Mitu believed that an internship was an extremely critical part of the job-hunting process. It meant getting your foot in the door and having a chance to convert it into a full-time offer. After much pleading, hard-selling and cajoling firms for internships, the options in front of Mitu weren't anything to write home about.

Mitu had taken for granted that internships just happen. Never in his wildest dreams did he imagine that he would have to struggle at every stage of his MBA experience.

There was minimal support from the school. All his struggles in this arena were driven by personal initiative. Unfortunately, none of the internships options in the pipeline materialized. He was finally offered the position of *Careers' Fellow* for 20 hours a week in his own school. Mitu explained the role – 'I'll be working with junior MBAs and helping them chart out a career plan... while I'm struggling with mine. Ironic, huh? It'll bring in some extra cash and the role involves profile reviews, mock interviews, etc. But I look at it as a way to continue networking with the next group of students.'

But Mitu also had a few unanswered questions in his mind. 'If the MBA programme is so intense, how come people find the time to work part-time? Twenty hours per week is no joke, considering that a normal 9 to 5 schedule in a five-day (Monday-

Friday) work environment amounts to forty hours. I would've rather looked at a regular full-time job and a part-time MBA. At least I wouldn't have exchanged my 100K annual salary to work part-time for peanuts.'

A Symbiotic Relationship?

The reasons why MBA candidates choose to do an internship are quite obvious. There is the chance to apply, in the real world, the new skills they have acquired in the classroom. There's also the career angle to it. There's always the possibility of an internship turning into a full-time role. The additional income earned by cash-strapped students during internship is always welcome, as some companies (such as management consulting firms) are known to be pretty generous with their compensation. It is also a good break from the lectures, assignments and evaluations.

But have you thought about it from a company's point of view? Why would they host an outsider for three months at their own cost? Companies are very possessive about their resources. When we say resources, we are talking about office space, computers/laptops, managerial time, canteen facilities, utilities/power, corporate image and several intangible aspects. Growing companies constantly struggle with the growing demand for these resources. If the company is located in a major commercial hub, the rental costs for a small area in prime locations can reach dizzying heights.

Let's face it. Unless the MBA has prior experience in the area of the internship opportunity, the productivity levels will not be very high, especially in the first few weeks. The intern would require considerable amounts of supervision and training. For this reason, companies that have frequently hosted interns realize the importance of assigning a mentor to guide their efforts and help them settle into the new environment. This investment of time and energy is a huge drain on the managers' own resources and can have an impact on their personal commitments. In most cases, internships do not form part of the managers' evaluation framework. This means the managers will not gain any mileage out of the free training and education that you get. The upside is limited and the downside is substantial. If you do not perform, they look bad.

Then there are issues related to confidentiality. Though you are made to sign a piece of paper with a fancy name (non-disclosure agreement or confidentiality agreement), the fact remains that an outsider has access to the company's deep dark secrets. Unlike in the case of an employee, the company does not usually carry out a detailed background check on an intern.

INTERNSHIP VARIATIONS

The 'regular' internship process may appear straightforward. You've got a target industry in mind that you want to break into. You talk to the internship coordinator in the campus to find out if there are opportunities that might be of interest to you from a long-term career perspective. If they do, fantastic! It makes life so much easier. You express your interest and submit an application. However, there may be other students from your own class who might be vying for this opportunity. If the company that has offered the internship has also approached other B-schools, then the level of competition is obviously higher. The positive part of such internships is that the company has thought through the process. They have a clear-cut plan in place, relatively speaking, once the intern joins them. They may have had a long-standing relationship with your B-school. This means, if you get through, you also have a first shot at any permanent positions that open up after the internship period has been completed. Usually, if companies have a new position to be filled up, interns who have successfully completed their mandated responsibilities and have impressed their supervisors stand a good chance of being considered.

If the company of your choice hasn't approached your B-school with a ready list of projects, do not despair. You can still approach companies directly to check if they could offer you something relevant. Cold-calling isn't the best way to do this, but after all the warm introductions have been exhausted, it may be inevitable. You might want to have a few project proposals ready. It could be anything that you can do relatively independently and something that adds value to their business, without interfering too much with their day-to-day schedules or overloading their resources.

Most employees in companies struggle to achieve a balance between the urgent and the important. Activities that fall under the *urgent* category include phone calls, ad hoc requests from the boss, an important customer hyperventilating and making a mountain out of a molehill. The *important* category of activities include those that may results in benefits in the longer term. Some examples of these would be include training, picking up new skills, planning for the future, improving processes, increasing efficiency, reducing waste. Most of these are strategic in nature and the general assumption across the corporate landscape is that the senior management is expected to take care of these areas. This may not necessarily be true.

Most of their energy is spent fire-fighting. New issues that were expected to be resolved yesterday suddenly appear out of nowhere.

Think of what you can do that will help the management address some of the *important* areas. A market entry study, a new business initiative, a feasibility study for a new product or service, cost-saving initiatives (always an item on the corporate agenda). If you can demonstrate that your proposals have a significant upside if the project is successful and a limited downside in case it falls flat on its face, you will get the attention of the company management. Of course, the expectations from the project have to be at a practical level.

Of course, you don't need to limit yourself to companies in and around the B-school campus. You can take up internship options in a different city or a different country or a different continent. It not only gives you a chance to experience life in the corporate lane, but also take in the sights, sounds and smells of a new culture. If you are successful in negotiating such a deal, the sponsoring company would be willing to pay for your travel, lodging and boarding expenses. They may also throw in an attractive stipend to cover your costs during your stay with them.

There is also another unusual approach to internships, which is to choose a field and an industry that you'd never want to get into for the rest of your working life. Why would anyone do that and mess up a perfectly legitimate chance at developing contacts and relationships in an area that you want to get into?

For one, because an MBA is also about experimentation. This may be your only chance to experiment with something that you will never come close to after you graduate from the MBA programme. As a student, career change is a permissible, and not to mention, a highly sought-after goal for several candidates. You are allowed liberties to explore careers without being bombarded with too many questions. As long as you have a logical and coherent explanation ready, you'll do just fine. You did it during your MBA application, didn't you?

For all you know, during internship in a field that you never wanted to get into, you could activate a dormant flair for the subject. Initially you might have picked up this unusual field because of your curiosity – or maybe because all the popular options had been taken up and this was the only industry where you faced little competition – but after spending three months in this arena, you realize that there's more to it than meets the eye. You become conscious of opportunities you thought never existed. After all, an MBA is about being flexible and open-minded.

So is an internship one of the unique selling propositions of an MBA programme?

Internship periods are a good way to put some of the theoretical concepts from class into practice. Again, as in the case of classroom lectures, time constraints can spoil the party here as well. The scope, format and time-frame of the internship make it impractical for many interns (especially those dragging their feet in an ill-designed internship programme) to do anything of real value – neither for the company, nor for themselves. In any case, an internship that pays zilch or a little over minimum wages (the best ones have already been lapped up by the super-achievers, remember?) is not the end in itself. At best, look at it as a networking opportunity.

9   Career Hunt

Nearly all MBA candidates in a good school have earned their seats because of their good credentials. Stop rolling your eyes, I said *nearly*, didn't I? Apart from academics, this also includes their professional accomplishments. Many would've worked in firms that are leaders in their domains, handled critical responsibilities in various functions and delivered solid results that earned them praise (and good bonuses).

Leaving a stable job for a degree is a risky proposition in itself. It can also be a daunting prospect, if you consider that you are putting yourself at the mercy of others – including the careers team, employers, alumni and headhunters – for landing a new job. A backup plan for many is the consoling thought that their pre-MBA employer has kept their doors open for them, in case they decide to come back to them. For others, even this is not an option, considering the bad blood that flowed after they announced their intention of quitting.

Even if an MBA candidate's objective is to get back into the industry and role that they originally came from, there are still benchmarks that need to be crossed. At the very minimum, these benchmarks could be related to company brand, salary and designation. Most MBA graduates would be reluctant to join a company that has lesser brand value than their pre-MBA companies (unless they decide to go the entrepreneurial route to start or join new ventures and start-ups), or pays less than their earlier roles, or needs them to join at levels that are relatively junior. For career-changers, the situation is a little different, and we'll cover that soon. But for the others, the bar gets raised higher the minute they get admitted to B-school or perhaps even before that.

Whatever might be the motive, the list of impediments to achieving career goals for many seems to be quite long, the biggest one being the setting up of impractical targets. Take Mitu's case, for instance. His job hunt had started early. He had realized it wasn't going to be a cakewalk, contrary to whatever statistics the school's website implied. But he hadn't expected that the road to his dream job would be so steep. He initially followed the general advice that he had received from his career mentors – 'Be focused. Close your eyes and think of what you want to do in life. Think of what gives you joy and pleasure. Now open your eyes. Your inner voice has given you the answer. This is the path you have to choose. Now that you know which industry you want to work in, shortlist the companies in this field that you want to target.'

So Mitu did what he was told, he closed his eyes, and now he had an answer that made his mentors happy. Management consulting. Yes, this is what he was born to do. This was his calling. He had no problem shortlisting the top five consulting firms that he would target. He was pleasantly surprised to see that 30 per cent of his classmates shared his vision! They all had the same names on their list as well. 'Great minds think alike,' he thought, and patted himself on his back.

He attended all the events that were sponsored for MBAs by these firms – the case-study workshops, the competitions, the question-and-answer sessions. He saw the same corporate faces at most of the events. That gave him a lot of confidence. The movers and shakers at all the top firms already knew him. Recruitment was now more or less a formality, Mitu was convinced. And then came the moment of reckoning. He typed out his formal application, proof-read it thoroughly, crossed his fingers and then hit on the submit button online. Or maybe he hit the submit button first and then crossed his fingers. Either way, he did all that he felt was right and was told to do by the guiding light. Then he did what 30 per cent of his class did. He waited for a response. Several months later, he got rejection letters from all the five firms he had applied to.

'So what?' his mentors said. They were always there to console his bruised ego. 'They aren't the only consulting firms in the country. Try tier-2 and tier-3 firms now. You may have a better shot.'

Mitu wasn't going to give up so easily. He applied to fifteen more consulting firms. He hit the submit button and crossed his fingers again (Yesss! got the sequence right this time). And he waited again. Some of his classmates suggested that he follow up with the firms to see what was happening. Unlike the top-five firms, the tier-2 and tier-3 firms had no structured MBA recruitment programmes with pre-defined dates and milestones. So after waiting for several weeks, it would be ok to call them, he was told.

'Hello, Mr Fox. Good morning. This is Mitu.'

'Mitu who?'

'Mitendra Lamba. We met twelve times earlier, when you came over for those MBA events at Bizcool.'

'Bizcool what?'

'Yes, Bizcool's the name of our business school. It offers MBA programmes.'

'MBA wha...?'

'You don't remember any of this? Anyway, never mind. I applied for the position of consultant in your firm, eight weeks back. As I haven't heard back from you, I thought I should give you a call to find out.'

'Oh...very sorry about the delay in responding. Our team has been extremely busy. Let me check internally and get back to you if there's any interest.'

'Thanks a ton, Mr Fox. Can I check back with you in a couple of days?'

'I wouldn't recommend that. We don't work well under pressure. Don't call us. We'll call you…like I said…*if* there's interest.'

'Thanks, Mr Fox…I really apprecia…' Click. Mitu heard the phone being disconnected at the other end, before he could complete his sentence. That was ok. Consultants were busy people. Mr Fox must have visited umpteen campuses and spoken with hundreds of candidates. You can't expect him to remember everything. After joining them, Mitu would probably be strapped for time as well.

Mitu almost felt guilty for having taken up precious minutes from Mr Fox's schedule. In that time, he'd have possibly saved a few millions rupees for a client, if he hadn't been talking to Mitu.

The patience paid off. Mitu finally got an interview call from *Consultants to International Corporates Incorporated* (Constipate Inc in short). Not a big firm. A boutique consultancy operating in a niche space. Which meant a smaller, close-knit and more intimate team. All good for Mitu. He would've got lost in a big firm anyway and he was never good with maps. There was no point in running behind big brands just for the heck of it. It was better to be a big fish in a small pond. But why fish? Wasn't this a rat-race? But we are digressing again.

'Look on the brighter side,' the guiding light told him. 'You could make it to Partner position in five years instead of ten.'

Mitu cracked, nay, demolished the initial telephonic interview he had with a junior consultant. He was called for a full-day recruitment session and then had to analyse a case study.

This time the wait wasn't too long. His rejection letter reached his home before he did.

There was something seriously wrong with the close-your-eyes-and-think methodology. Also, the focused approach seemed to be pretty ineffective and wasn't yielding results. Mitu decided to expand his horizon (one of the reasons for pursuing an MBA) and include a few more careers that he had ignored. In the era of machine guns, Mitu was still using an old shotgun. The job market was an ocean and he just needed to have a bigger net and cast it wider. So he went for a strategy upgrade and sent out his resume to all companies, in all industries, in all countries that have English as one of their official languages. Mitu has since hit the submit button so many times, he can no longer cross his fingers. They hurt from overuse.

Unless a company is looking for highly unique and specialized skills that you possess, be ready for stiff competition during your job hunt. In almost all mainstream professions, there are more employees struggling for a few good jobs than you can imagine. Also, with geographical constraints dissolving rapidly and with more people willing to relocate for the right role, the supply pools for such opportunities become vast. Your strong alumni network within the company may make it easier for your resume to float to the top of the applicant pile, but the rest of the journey still remains to be traversed. If an employer has to choose between a non-MBA with the right experience (and you can be dead sure that this species does exist) and an absolute greenhorn from a top B-school (or someone with limited experience in the field), the choice is pretty clear. In most cases, however, there will be many who have both – the experience as well as the qualifications.

For the urgent positions, the employer will be less likely to wait for six more months till you finish your academic commitments. If they can find someone who can join in a week's time or in a month, they'd make that offer right there. The show and the business must go on, right?

CAREER HUNT ◀ 111

If you are an Indian candidate hoping to land a plum job in foreign-land, there are other kind of hassles (or challenges, as you'll learn to call them). For starters, you'll need a work permit. And for your prospective employer that means not just a substantial amount of money to be pumped in (dealing with immigration lawyers who charge on an hourly basis) but also a whole lot of paperwork and legwork. Bigger companies that have been recruiting MBAs from the good schools would have the processes and the infrastructure in place to manage this annually. But everyone will not be as enthusiastic to get you on board when they can get local resources cheaper and faster. Plus there's the pressure on recruiting firms to give preference to local talent before considering international applicants.

Some roles might have a cultural bias. For instance, if you are getting into a marketing role where you are expected to connect with your clients (prospective and existing) before you can see a sale happening, then you'd better know what it takes to establish that rapport. As a cricket-enthusiast, if you start showing off your knowledge about Tendulkar's world-class statistics during business meetings, expect a blank stare from the multimillionaire American client you want that contract from. If you've grown up watching NBA, NFL or MLB, you'd still be able to hold a mutually interesting conversation. But if these acronyms sound like Greek and Latin to you, probably you are in the wrong role.

Issues related to dignity of labour can also throw a spanner in the works. 'How can they expect a top MBA graduate to do THAT work?' Ego issues can put a whole lot of opportunities (even if it was meant to be something you take up to tide over the difficult times) out of reach for the perceived stigma those roles will carry if the news were to reach back home to your native place.

Staying back in the US (or any other country) is an issue with your temporary work permit (Optional Practical Training or

OPT, as it's called in the US) reaching its end date. Coming back could be a bigger issue if you have a big loan on your head. An Indian salary may not be sufficient to pay back the dollar loan. And the fact that many Indian employers will not entertain your calls, can come as a rude wake-up call. 'You have a nice profile,' they might say over email. 'Let's take this forward when you return as it's a little difficult for us to do this when you are in a different continent and there's no timeline yet about when you are going to get back.'

Another concern in your head is the social awkwardness of dealing with nosy relatives and neighbours and (again a perceived) loss of face if you go back. 'You couldn't even find a decent job out there in the land of opportunities?'

Recessions make the situation even trickier, as discussed below.

IMPLICATIONS OF BUSINESS CYCLES

The recent recession caused a lot of turmoil not just in the US and Europe, but also in Asia. Though the impact in India wasn't as brutal as in the West, the damage was there for everyone to see. Company sales were way below target, many planned projects requiring heavy capital investment were held back indefinitely, and we realized we aren't as insulated from the global worries as we thought. International companies started laying off employees in India as well, to reduce costs. This also meant domestic companies enforced a hiring freeze and many good guys got retrenched. The workload for the retained guys went up and they were expected to grin and bear it as they still had their jobs.

During a slowdown, one prime way of cutting costs is SG&A. It stands for selling, general & administrative expense. Business-class travel is replaced by economy-class travel or sometimes No Travel, depending on how strict the company policies are. You may need a top manager to approve all travel requisitions. SG&A includes salary expenses as well. This would mean a freeze on hiring, reduced or nil increments and bonuses. Companies also don't shy away from using another lethal weapon in their arsenal, yes, the dreaded 'L' word – layoffs.

Consider the case of investment bankers. They have always been the blue-eyed boys chasing million-dollar dreams in the high-stake, high-octane world of finance. And then a bolt from the blue in the form of the global credit crunch hit them. Newspapers carrying sensational headlines announced how top investment banks had started laying off staff. The dramatically inclined ones also carried photographs of employees walking out of glass and chrome buildings with brown boxes containing their personal belongings. Many of those who had been laid off had very specialized skills in niche areas ranging from structuring CDOs[1] to risk-management applications.

Timing the Markets

Many employees facing the heat of recession start considering B-schools as an option to weather the storm. The intention is to spend two years in a productive manner by gaining new skills and a strong qualification.

The other option is to try and secure another job. However, this approach can turn out to be even more frustrating, almost like trying to flow against the current. There are too many overqualified candidates vying for the same miniscule number of good jobs. Even after landing a good job, there still is no guarantee that the new company will not have SG&A reduction plans on its agenda. So, in comparison, the MBA option does seem better. But it is an expensive option. If you can pull it off, you can heave

---

[1] Collateralized debt obligations (CDOs) are an unregulated type of asset-backed security and structured credit product (*source:* Wikipedia).

a sigh of relief after four years (one year of applications, two years in B-school and one year in a stable job). As a strategy, it does look appealing.

What puts the whole thing out of whack is the unpredictability of economic cycles. Ask any economist. Many will have their own theories about what happened and what could happen.

Also, watch out for the reverse possibilities. Many students who join MBA programmes when the economy is buoyant realize during the course that they are staring at a looming recession just when they are about to graduate. None of this happens abruptly. Cycles take their sweet time to become apparent. In the middle of a full-blown recession, it isn't uncommon to see two articles in rival publications arguing whether the economic parameters convincingly prove that the world is in recession or not. Several months later, when everyone gets tired of debating over how deep we are in recession, it's time to launch a new topic – When are we most likely to come out of recession? And it's not only economists who have a say in this. Everyone worth his salt wants to pool in with their two bits – academicians, educators, businessmen, astrologers, actors – the list goes on.

At the time of writing this book, the global business environment is still in the process of a slow, painful recovery. After many months of graduation, several MBA graduates (including those from the top schools), are still struggling to find a foothold in the job market. All this after tapping into the regular resources – alumni networks, the school's career services team, online job portals, cold-calling employers, head-hunters, the works. They are all highly intelligent candidates who'd surely have spent countless hours weighing the pros and cons of their decision. But who knew the economy would turn the way it did?

10 Career Change

Career change is the most difficult to achieve and also one of the reasons why many professionals choose to get back to school. This is why most B-schools have a special section on their careers' page dedicated to those who have successfully managed to switch lanes. The motivations for this may be many. Some might want to get into professions that pay more, appear more glamorous, provide a better work/life balance or help in building new skills and networks. There may be others who are just too frustrated with their current professions and do not care where they end up as long as it is away from their current industry.

Here are some of the popular destinations on the wish-list of MBA applicants looking for a career change.

TECHNOLOGY

This might be familiar territory for most readers as a majority of MBA candidates from India fall in this pool. Not everyone wants to move out of the technology industry per se. Many might be happy transitioning out of their technical roles into opportunities that get them closer to the business. Despite the dotcom shakeout, it is still an industry with a lot of promise and Indians have a leg up in the race.

By technology, we are referring to hardware and software. Stuff that you can see and touch directly and stuff that works behind the scenes to ensure you live a life that is a considerable improvement on the past. The gargantuan scope and ever-expanding nature of this field opens up a multitude of careers. Information Technology, a subset of this, has been a favourite destination for many MBAs. After the dotcom bust, entrepreneurs realized it wasn't enough just to have a fantastic idea that no one else had come up with. They also needed to convince investors that the concept was economically viable. Many of the new Internet-based businesses based more on adrenaline than on solid business plans have disappeared from the technology landscape. The ones that have managed to survive have come out stronger. With moderated and recalibrated expectations, the growth targets and the actual achievements finally began falling in sync. The concept of incubation centres is catching on abroad and in India. IIMs and IITs have incubation centres for budding entrepreneurs. For instances, the Society for Innovation and Entrepreneurship (SINE) based out of IITB is a technology incubator that provides support services to early-stage businesses with growth potential. These incubation arrangements are generally for a fixed period of time (for example, three years) beyond which the incubatee companies are expected to move out and fend for themselves. However, one of the pre-requisites for getting into SINE is a linkage with IITB. If you don't have that linkage you'd have to hunt for other incubators willing to host you.

But that's just one part of the picture. There's a tremendous amount of investment in technology mode by large corporations to ensure that their operations continue without any hiccups. A downtime of a few hours could potentially cause a loss of several hundred thousand or even millions of dollars in lost revenue. This includes systems and software applications such as Enterprise Resource Planning (ERP), Customer Relationship Management (CRM), Supply Chain Management (SCM) and Management Information Systems (MIS). The first massive investment required for such systems is in the area of servers, networks, PCs/laptops. It also includes software customization, installation, testing and roll-out. This is just the one-time cost. Additionally there's also the recurring cost of maintaining, upgrading, trouble-shooting these expensive systems on a regular basis. Each of these areas is a potential career option. If you are planning to enter the technical areas, an MBA degree is not a pre-requisite. It would help if you can proudly display your repertoire of certifications in various areas of expertise – J2EE, .NET (pronounced Dot-Net), SAP, Networking.

Many firms encourage rotations across the technology platform. This is hugely beneficial for gaining well-rounded skills as it gives you the chance to evaluate project management roles and lead assignments that use a variety of technologies. Even when you do get into a project management position, a PMI certification[1] would probably help you more than an MBA degree. In fact, many organizations view this as a pre-requisite for all their new project managers. The companies are going to sell your credentials to the client and try to build credibility for their organization by putting your certifications and experience in specific technology disciplines. If you join a project as a consultant or a contractor, you might be expected to spend extended durations at the client's premises.

INVESTMENT BANKING

The work done by investment banks can roughly be broken up into two areas: Corporate Finance and Sales & Trading. The former involves providing financial advice and support to corporations considering mergers, acquisitions, divestitures, raising capital through initial public offerings (IPOs) and any other corporate restructuring strategies. In many cases, the term investment banking is used to refer to corporate finance. It's all

[1] http://www.pmi.org/careerdevelopment/pages/obtaining-credential. aspx#pmp

about the deal. This is a fast-paced, high-octane environment where bankers are expected to juggle multiple transactions.

In an acquisition transaction, for instance, the job involves identifying potential targets, working on pitch books, presenting these to the client, valuing them and attaching a price tag, approaching the target and negotiating the deal on behalf of the client, looking into the legal agreements, evaluating options (including raising funds) to finance the deal and actually executing the deal. Endless hours are spent on analysing financial statements (balance sheets, profit and loss accounts) and working on financial models (valuations, cash flows, equity/ debt structuring for the acquired entity) that depict best-case and worst-case scenarios for the business. As a green-faced fresher, you may spend a lot of time behind computers churning out the numbers and supporting data, while your seniors will be part of the power meetings in the client's boardroom. For most bankers, the adrenaline rush that comes with seeing a deal that they've worked on in the newspaper headlines makes it all worth the effort. And yes, another aspect that makes it all worth it – the salaries.

Sales & Trading involves buying and selling equity and debt securities to institutional buyers. Though the aggressiveness and urgency in the nature of work is similar to that in Corporate Finance, what sets it apart is that it is time-bound. When the markets close, the traders get to switch off their terminals and go home, unlike Corporate Finance guys who are expected to be 'on-call' 24×7. In the area of Sales & Trading, there are also numerous jobs in the mid-office and back-office side. This may include technology, risk management, research and settlement.

Investment banks are usually categorized into the big bulge-bracket firms (like Goldman Sachs, Merrill Lynch, J.P. Morgan) and the smaller boutique firms that provide a subset of services and focus on specific industries.

The first two to three years are the most gruelling as analysts go through the never ending and always thankless lists of menial tasks. Some quit to join B-school while those who've already completed B-school decide to stick on for a few years more. Many bankers proudly brag about their hundred-hour weeks and their glamorous lifestyles. However, the high-burnout rate also means that most bankers leave investment banking to join the industry (usually one of their former clients) in senior positions.

Two books are recommended for anyone considering a career in investment banking: *Monkey Business – Swinging Through the Wall Street Jungle* by John Rolfe & Peter Troob, who capture the frustrations, the chaos and the idiosyncrasies of the investment banking industry, and *Liar's Poker* by Michael Lewis, who describes his experiences on Wall Street as a bond trader.

Sensing the growing demand for domestic investment banking jobs, a new breed of institutions is coming up in India to train candidates in investment banking concepts and theory. One such example is the School of Investment Banking (SIB). It offers short-term courses and placement assistance in investment banks and KPOs. The kind of career options vary though and may not be the ones you are targeting. But if you are looking for a break in the Indian investment banking industry, it might be a quicker and cheaper way to get in.

ACCOUNTING/ASSURANCE/ADVISORY

These are the formally dressed strangers we see lurking around the corridors, cubicles and offices in most corporations, while the rest of the staff is dressed in casuals. They work for professional services firms (the Big 4), so they have to look like professionals.

We are talking about firms such as Ernst & Young, PricewaterhouseCoopers, KPMG and Deloitte. Arthur Andersen was another firm that was part of this league (in the Big-5 days).

It went down after the infamous Enron scandal that rocked the accounting world. Prestige and credibility can mean everything for professional service firms. However, though the Enron affair shook the credibility of accounting firms, it did not sound their death knell. In fact, many ironically noted that the accounting industry (which, according to them, was responsible for the downfall of some real big names in the corporate world) was called back by the very same corporate world to implement stricter controls.

A significant part of the revenue for these firms comes from audit assignments, or 'Assurance' as it is known within the industry. But that's not the only thing they do. They are also involved in tax-related and transaction advisory services (valuations, due diligence, tax optimization, deal structuring in case of mergers and acquisitions). Another lucrative business area these firms got into was business consulting. However, due to conflict of interest issues, the consulting divisions were hived off into separate entities or sold off.

The experience gained by accounting and finance professionals in these organizations is considered to be invaluable, as auditors and consultants are exposed to a lot of businesses in a short span of time.

You could be working as an internal auditor, management accountant or in the area of forensic audit. Then there are a host of new areas such as Sarbanes Oxley (SOX) implementation where these firms are doing business. Accounting standards keep getting updated, new standards get introduced, and new regulations are initiated that corporations have to abide by. Accounting professionals need to keep themselves abreast of all such developments. A focused professional qualification such as the Certified Public Accountant (CPA) may be looked upon more favourably than a generic qualification such as an MBA.

The journey from entry in the organization to being promoted to partner position can be quite long (around ten years, if you are lucky) and along the way, you'll have to bear all that a big firm has to dish out – politics and bureaucracy being the top two offerings. While working on assignments, the hours can be long, but unlike investment banking and management consulting, the incentives for putting in late hours are limited. Employee turnover in these organizations is high and accounting firms are always on the lookout for fresh talent. Other than the Big-4, there are other firms like BDO and Grant Thornton operating in this space.

MANAGEMENT CONSULTING

You are honest in admitting to yourself that you haven't really finalized any specific career path. What if you do interesting work and make some good money for a few years while you continue to contemplate on that one great industry or company you want to work for? For several decades, many fresh undergraduates and MBAs across countries seemed to think Management Consulting offered that flexibility. We are specifically talking about strategy consulting firms like McKinsey, The Boston Consulting Group (BCG) and Bain & Company. Apart from these top-tier firms, there's a range of boutique consulting firms that focus on specific industries and geographies. Some of these may not be as well-known as the top firms, but the variety of work they take on can be equally diverse and challenging.

Why would any company engage external consultants to look into their deepest darkest secrets and recommend plans for the future? Well, for starters, consultants are expected to bring in an outsider's perspective. For organizations that have been operating in a particular industry for several years, it is very easy to start developing tunnel vision. Strategies and processes that have worked for them over the years continue to seem like the best bet to take them into the future as well. Such organizations feel that the management consulting firms that have helped solve problems for multiple companies (including competing firms at some point in time) have *been there and done that* so many times that they have a better probability of suggesting solutions with a higher chance of success.

Another aspect is that the regular employees, who spend most of their time firefighting and attending to daily chores, may also lack the specific capabilities to effectively tackle the specific organizational issues that the senior management wants to address. Sample assignments may include strategies to introduce a new product in the market, to expand the company's geographical presence within and outside the country, to evaluate the possibilities of partnering with other organizations with complementing products, to consider the possibility of hiving off a business unit that may be making losses or is no longer part of the core-competencies (apologies for the buzzword) of the company. Consultants could also be brought in by a company's management to act as the bad cops and execute unpleasant tasks (such as layoffs) that the company's management would shy away from. During the course of the assignment, consultants usually work on the site, that is, on the client's premises. This means a Monday-to-Friday travel schedule isn't uncommon and during peak times, the number of hours that consultants spend in the office may be quite considerable. This also means they have little time for personal and social life. The perks? Well, you could get to travel to glamorous locations, stay in five-star hotels, hobnob with CEO-level executives within client organizations, travel business class and pile up on those frequent flyer miles. The salaries are much higher than in other industries. Newbies join in as analyst (pre-MBA positions) and work their way up to partnership. Along the way, depending on the firm they work for, they'll change labels like associate, consultant, senior/principal consultant, manager, associate director, director, etc. However, though salaries and bonuses are quite substantial, relative to other industries, they could pale in comparison to investment banking compensation packages, especially in boom time. Many consultants move on to join former clients where they've already established a good rapport with the senior management and an intimate understanding of the company business and culture. This is a common exit route for many consultants.

Human Resources

'I am a people person.' Sounds familiar? You hear it all the time and at times from unexpected quarters. But it takes more than just being a people person to be a successful professional in the HR department. Their work goes way beyond recruitment and coordinating annual appraisals. Getting fresh blood into the organization is definitely one of the key roles of HR executives. But their to-do list includes several other critical areas. Viewing people as *resources* gives it a whole new meaning. Like any other resource, there's the need to

- *Ramp employees up or scale them down*
  This covers the entire gamut of hiring fresh graduates, experienced hands or urgently replacing a key position that has been vacated. Hiring can be a long, painful and often frustrating cycle as it involves shortlisting candidates (either directly by tapping into their own resume database or using external placement agencies), carrying out interviews, a battery of tests (aptitude, psychometric, technical), passing on feedback and making final recommendations.
  It also includes managing the complete exit cycle (due to resignations or if the company has asked employees to leave).

- *Measure and monitor if employees are generating output as desired on a continuous basis*

  This is where the appraisal process fits in. It involves setting challenging yet practical targets for each employee in conjunction with their superiors at the beginning of the monitoring period (this may be an annual or six-monthly process). At the end of the monitoring period, the preset targets are compared to what has been achieved. The variable component of the salary is usually tied to this. Depending on whether the employee has failed to meet, met or surpassed expectations, the incentives get calculated.

- *Ensure employees are provided with incentives to perform*

  This would include designing the salary structures (including bonus schemes), putting in place and running pension schemes, designing ESOP (employee stock options plans) to ensure key employees are retained, recognizing and awarding star players within the team.

- *Provide employees with tools, techniques and skills to be more effective in their current roles or take on more responsibility in the near future*

  The HR team could introduce productivity enhancing tools, such as online forms (to manage leave applications, travel requisitions, suggestions, complaints).

  On the training side, the team would work in the areas of recognizing the technical, managerial or general training needs of employees programmes, coordinating with internal or external trainers, managing nominations, defining and customizing the structure of the course, incorporating feedback from attendees to ensure that the training courses are fine-tuned for effectiveness.

- *Organize and structure employees in the most effective manner*

In small flat organizations, this is not so much of an issue. However, as organizations gain mass and extend across locations, all corporate departments tend to get a little tricky to manage. This is when it becomes important to design an optimum team structure. For instance, there might be a regional structure with one central team and several smaller satellite teams spread across the main cities managing all HR activities around their region. Alternatively, in place of geography, the business units may drive the structure, with dedicated teams catering to the HR requirements of each sub-business. In most cases, for bigger organizations, it can be a matrix structure, that is, a combination of these two approaches.

PHILANTHROPY/NON-PROFIT/SOCIAL ENTERPRISES

With all the advancement in technology and science, is the world really better off today than it was several centuries back? Arguably, most of the big problems we face today – environment, hunger, poverty, health, inequality – have grown to their current proportions in the last hundred years alone. Individuals and organizations are increasingly becoming aware of the seriousness of these issues and their implications. The impact is already being felt by the current generation and the whiplash will be worse for the coming generations.

The United Nations initiative – Millennium Development Goals – may be the largest organized attempt to deal with some of these problems. Many NGOs have embraced these initiatives and are already working on these at the grassroots level. Multilateral agencies such as the UN and governments have also taken them up at higher levels, such as policy formulation. The main perception that these thoughts and concepts are only for a handful of idealists with lofty but impractical visions of the future is slowly but surely changing.

This area also provides a fertile ground for fresh ideas. The concept of social enterprises (with a focus on environmental and social impact in addition to good old financial gains) is catching on. Several entrepreneurs have already taken the initiative to convert these challenges into opportunities and get all that they would expect from 'regular' business ventures and maybe, more. You might want to join one of the existing non-profit organizations or launch your own social enterprise.

Poverty

In the area of poverty alleviation, microfinance is considered by far the best tool available today (despite critical views) to address this issue. It involves making small loans (usually without any collateral) to poor people to launch their own microenterprises. This has opened up a whole new class of customers who never had access to credit earlier. In fact, apart from turning to traditional sources of funding such as banks, microfinance institutions are also exploring alternative sources of funding, including private equity funds, venture capitalists and High Networth Individuals (HNIs) with an inclination towards philanthropy. The model relies on group lending, which penalizes the entire group even if a single member defaults. Due to this the default rate has been very low. This combined with relatively high returns makes it an extremely encouraging asset class for mainstream investors. SKS recently became the first Indian microfinance institution to get listed on the stock exchange. A sign that microfinance institutions have arrived and are no longer waiting for their real world practicality to be confirmed. However, the scope and reach of such initiatives is still limited, considering the phenomenal bottom-of-the-pyramid potential India offers.

Environment

Start-ups working on commercializing concepts in the area of alternative energy sources, such as solar energy, wind energy and ethanol are also gaining attention. The stringent targets and deadlines faced by countries to reduce their carbon footprint have triggered this interest.

Food

Big strides in the area of leveraging technology and science in agriculture has meant that the entire supply chain – from producing crops, harvesting, storing, processing, distributing, providing access to big markets for small players – has undergone tremendous change.

Besides these, the areas of education and health provide ample opportunities for people with the right skills to make a positive difference.

Organizations operating in this space have realized that they need to bring in professional skills and capabilities, if they have to take it all to the next level.

PRIVATE EQUITY/VENTURE CAPITAL

Though these are two distinctly disparate professions, they tend to be clubbed together. Private Equity (PE) is an umbrella term covering everything from early stage to late stage funding of companies that are not publicly traded,[2] while Venture Capital (VC) is primarily concerned with early stage investments. In order words, VC is a subset of PE. These funds generally comprise small teams with a few general partners and a small team of supporting staff, including associates, principals and administrative assistants. General Partners (GPs) approach

[2] PIPE deals (Private investment in public enterprises) are an exception to this rule.

investors (called Limited Partners) and raise funds. Some of these funds are industry specific while others are industry agnostic. Once the target size of the fund is reached, GPs identify investment opportunities with the help of their supporting teams. These target companies are usually mature organizations with a proven business model, where the PE fund sees growth opportunity. Depending on the stake in an invested company, the PE fund may ask for a board seat to oversee that the company continues to cruise in the mutually agreed direction. Operating styles of PE funds vary considerably. Some follow a hands-off approach, assuming that the existing management is in the best position to continue growing the business. Others may take a hands-on approach in the belief that they can bring more than just capital into the business. This *something more* may include contacts within the industry to take the company into new markets, improve internal processes, consider 'inorganic' growth options by making one or more acquisitions.

There may also be a change in the top-level management, with PE funds getting their own guys to run the show on their behalf. These turnaround experts have a clear mandate and a definite timeframe in which to execute it. Unlike strategic acquisitions carried out by mainstream industry players, PE funds usually have limited patience levels and are always on the lookout for the best exit option for their investments in a predefined time. This may range from a few years to almost a decade. The latter might be more common in infrastructure-related investments where the gestation time is pretty long. ICICI Venture is India's biggest player in this field. There are also the Indian arms of several international PE funds, such as Carlyle and Blackstone.

Venture Capital, on the other hand, is a totally different ball game. The fund sizes and therefore the investment amounts in individual companies are much smaller (tens of million dollars as opposed to hundreds of million dollars in case of PE). Technology companies have been a favourite hunting ground for VC funds, though the VC model itself is not limited to this one industry. In many cases, the VC team looks for a proof of concept for a new product or service by the investee company, usually a start-up in its first few years of existence. There are a few niche players among VCs as well. Some, like Aavishkaar (a social rural Venture Capital firm founded by entrepreneur Vineet Rai) have been getting a lot of traction in their unconventional areas. So if you are a freshly minted MBA hoping to do some good work AND make money, there are newer opportunities coming up every day.

The skills sets required for PE and VC funds are quite different, though sterling academic credentials can help in both cases. A finance background helps in PE while an engineering background is usually what clicks for VC. PE funds usually attract investment bankers and senior executives with the right connections to raise new funds and execute deals for existing ones. VCs usually attract senior executives from technology firms. The other type of profile that will gain attention is that of an entrepreneur who has launched a start-up and actually driven it up the curve for handsome returns. In both PE as well as VC, at junior levels, you'll be doing loads of research and not as many deals as you'd like to.

As you'd have guessed, it's about a whole lot of superachievers or potential superachievers trying to become richer. No wonder every Tom, Dick and Harry wants to be part of the elite league, but not all of them will succeed.

A career change is one of the dream objectives for many who take up the MBA route. It is also the most difficult to achieve. This is where the calibre of the B-school comes into play. Some schools, over time, build up a reputation of being the favourite feeding ground for consulting firms or banking roles or industry jobs. Firms may come in and pick up dozens of students from such institutions.

All schools aren't as fortunate. For many, placing their graduating students in regular roles itself poses a formidable challenge, leave alone assisting them in an awe-inspiring career change. It isn't a pretty sight.

The nice-looking pie-charts on many B-school websites, proclaiming the impressive number of career-changers, hide the ordeal that most of the successful candidates have gone through to achieve this transition. I wish there were charts to show how many students who were originally aiming for a complete career change (or just a change in their function, industry or location), gave it their best, failed and resigned themselves to their fate. Those statistics would be interesting to look at.

For popular career options, MBA candidates have to compete with students of their own class, those from other institutions, experienced candidates with extensive industry knowledge exploring new avenues, internal employees of the firm looking for internal mobility. For the career options listed in this chapter, the demand invariably overshadows the supply of good roles, irrespective of the state of the economy.

When you are playing the risk-reward game, you might want to keep in mind a paraphrased axiom – a good job in hand today could be worth more than an uncertain (and unguaranteed) job after the MBA.

But now that you have been cautioned, I should also add that many candidates have successfully managed career transitions using their MBA to get a foot in the door. So if you are extremely driven then you should do it head on. The right B-school can be your best partner and propel you in the right direction.

11 So What's Your Goal?

What is it that you really wanted when you started researching for MBA schools? Knowledge? Money? A new career? But in your quest for one or more of these, did you get starry-eyed about all the other bonuses that business schools offered?

We know we can please some people some of the time, but not all the people all the time. Are MBA programmes trying to do the latter by offering a mind-boggling array of options – the choice of electives, special interest groups, wide career options, an impressive alumni network, etc? Do they attempt to be everything for everyone enrolling in their courses? Is there a basic flaw in the underlying philosophy itself?

While you ponder that question, here are a few alternatives to the MBA if your goals are limited to one or more of the following:

KNOWLEDGE

a. Books

Artefact A (Human Beings): The earliest form of modern man made an appearance on earth some 200,000 years back.

Artefact B (Books): If we ignore ancient forms of writing systems, alphabetical writing made a presence some 4,000 years back.

Artefact C (MBA): About a hundred years old.

In recording, storing and transferring of knowledge across

generations, note that Artefact A has predominantly been dependent on Artefact B.

Artefact C is a baby in comparison, and is itself dependent to a large extent on Artefact B for knowledge transfer. So it's more an agent, a middleman, a conduit in your quest for knowledge.

So, all in all, books are your best bet if you are looking purely for knowledge and new concepts. Make sure you pick the right list of books. Appendix B should help you get started in this area.

b. Internet

In a conversation, you are less likely to use the question 'Do you have an Internet connection?' It'll probably be on the lines of, 'So you have got broadband or dial-up?' And it's high time you stopped using it just for playing multi-user Internet games, surfing dirty sites and downloading movies and songs.

Focus instead on the text-only sites (Tip: In your Internet browser, switch off the *Show Pictures* option using Tools-options-advanced settings) and read more about what's happening in the real world. The amount of freely available information on the Internet can be intimidating and unnerving at the same time. The concept of hyperlinks (links to other pages) ensures that you'll never start and end an Internet session on the same page. That's where the discipline comes in. Pick a topic of your choice and do an initial search on it using Google, Yahoo or any other search engine. Chances are you'll be bombarded with links to websites that cover this topic. Fortunately, these are sorted by relevance, popularity, etc. So take a look at the results displayed on the first few pages and jump to those sites. Choose those that provide a high-level overview of the topic instead of getting into unnecessary details. Discover the tip of the iceberg before trying to see what lies below. This is all the more important in areas where you have no preliminary background. You don't want to be turned off by too much technicality on day one. If the topic continues to sustain your interest, your inquisitiveness will automatically take you towards its finer nuances.

c. Subject Specific Courses

There are specialized courses available on almost every imaginable topic – whether it is fashion, computers, investing, photography, designing or art appreciation. If there's a university or educational institution close by, check out their short-term and long-term courses. These may either be delivered by the same faculty that teaches the full-fledged degree programmes or they may be conducted by guest faculty invited from the industry. See if you can get access to the rest of the resources (like the library, academic databases) of the institution. Find out if you will earn credits for these courses that you could utilize in case you decide to pursue the main course. When you are on campus, strike up a conversation with the full-time students and see how different life is and will be for them. What are the new developments in the area of your interest, who's doing what...in campus and outside? All these inputs might set the direction for you and help you decide if you should pursue a full-time programme or stay away from it.

If you are far away from the closest institution or university offering courses that you like, fret not, my friend. There may be alternative ways to gain that esoteric knowledge.

Check out the local clubs, yellow pages and classified ads in newspapers to find out if there are any courses being offered close to your area of residence or work. Most of them are usually intended for students or working people. The timings are also offered accordingly to make it flexible for this target group. Some may allow you to take breaks (to accommodate office trips, vacation, work-load spikes) and resume back when your schedule becomes more predictable. However, many are operated as mom-'n-pop shops and may differ considerably in terms of quality and credibility. Visit their premises to find out if they will serve your purpose.

d. Online/Correspondence Courses

Many of the courses that brick-and-mortar institutions offer may also be available as online courses. This may be a good option if your job doesn't allow you the luxury or liberty of joining a regular evening or weekend course. You might be spending too much time in office or college, and the additional commute to the nearest class may be killing.

Most of these courses provide a structured download of information that you are expected to absorb and digest. However, unlike the previous Internet approach (where you essentially structure your own course and there's no one to test whether you have grasped the basic elements of the topic), online courses and correspondence courses might have interactive elements to it. You might have to attend a few classroom sessions (either in person or using technology such as video-conferencing), and you may also get tested at the end of the course.

Only you can judge if you need to go in for an online course or are better off receiving personalized training.

CAREER CHANGE

a. Volunteering

A lot of businesses need legs, hands and brains to keep their wheels churning. Most of them are also strapped for cash. So much work to be done, not enough resources. Volunteering is your opportunity to contribute to a real business and also gain useful skills in return. Don't expect your retirement kitty to swell up after a few months or years of volunteering. You may not get any financial rewards for your contribution. The organization that you are volunteering for may offer a modest allowance to cover basic expenses like food and commuting. If you have been nominated for a position that requires specialized skills, you may even receive training in that area, before you actually start working. Volunteering is huge in the social sector.

If you already have specialized skills in any area – legal, finance, medical, administration, project management, research, analysis – there is an organization somewhere out there waiting for you to approach them as they desperately need your help.

As an example, check out the United Nations volunteers' website (http://www.unv.org/). It provides thousands of volunteering opportunities across the globe every year.

If you have already volunteered for an organization for a decent period of time, it signals to the rest of the market that you have useful skills that have been tried and tested in a real business. It means that the next organization recruiting you will not have to invest their precious energy and money to train you and ensure your productivity.

b. Join a Start-up

If you can't get into one of the bigger and reputed firms, there's no need to despair. There are a lot of smaller organizations doing some real good work in various fields. They may not have the resources, the marketing muscle or the budget to embark on a brand-building exercise yet. They may not have a properly structured volunteering programme. But they could be the next stars on the horizon. They are more easily approachable and you can possibly get an appointment directly with the company founder(s) and discuss how you could get involved in their business. Most start-ups are valued by the quality of their management and their employees. Of course, the industry in which they operate, their product and their competitive position are all important. But the criterion topmost on the list is – their people.

The best thing about start-ups is that there aren't any real pre-defined glass walls to constrain your potential. Key employees have the freedom and the flexibility to don many hats, based on the need of the organization. So even if you have been invited to join them for your fantastic programming skills, in a few weeks or months, you might find yourself working on a sales presentation or a product proposal or face-to-face with a potential client. The pay you'll get in a start-up may not be that great but the learning curve is steep, the pace is intense and the overall value of the experience is something you can only dream about in a bigger organization.

NETWORKING

a. Clubs

Trade fairs, seminars, workshops, associations and clubs offer a diverse range of opportunities to network. Whatever the subject – boating, positive thinking, biking, entrepreneurship or psychic healing – it isn't too difficult to come across a dedicated group of people who've been meeting formally or casually to discuss, debate and share information about their common interests. Many of these might offer free sessions during which they might try to sell their services.

Many of these may charge a nominal fee for membership and for the special events that they organize. You'll come across other excited souls interested in the subject. Some of these sessions may be held on a regular basis at a venue easily accessible to you.

This will bring you in contact with industry experts and also others who want to be associated with this topic in some form – suppliers, customers, academicians, students and businessmen. You'll become aware of the companies operating in this space, what they are looking for and what constraints they've been facing.

Make sure you exchange visiting cards with your contact information, so you can continue your dialogue offline, that is, after the formal events are over.

If you are at the right place at the right time, it may translate into business opportunities that you never expected.

b. Online Forums

If you aren't already on one or more of the online networking sites, you run the risk of being labelled *old-school*, *techno-challenged*, *uncool* or any of the several variations that fall in this category. There's a huge list of such sites vying for new members everyday. Some of them have several million registered members, dwarfing out the rest.

However, we've got to differentiate between their objectives. Some sites (like LinkedIn and XING) are predominantly for business and professional networking, whereas others (like Orkut and Facebook) are essentially social networking sites. Both options are a good way to get back in touch with old friends and colleagues and also to develop new connections. There's also a big variety of customized topic-specific networking sites for you to explore if you have a niche area in mind like music, books, dating, online games, motherhood, education, movies, languages and hobbies.

Here we'll focus on professional networking (which means no dating tips). The way the concept works is pretty simple. You create an account and get registered on the site, create a brief profile for yourself (sharing as little or as much as you want) and then start connecting with other users who already have profiles on the site. Why do that? For one, it lets you know what your contacts have been up to over the last few years since you last bumped into them. You can find out about their current profession, their current location, and everything else that is current about them. You can tap into their networks and get directly connected to friends of friends or colleagues of colleagues, if you think there may be mutual interest. There are security settings that decide how much you want your contacts to see as opposed to the rest of the world. Use it to contact interesting people and set up informational interviews.

c. Golf

On Mitu's first day in office, his company CEO was describing how his tastes and preferences had changed since he joined the firm. As a fresh graduate who just joined the company, he thoroughly enjoyed basketball. After a few years, he started developing an interest in baseball. After becoming the top boss of the company, he started taking a keen interest in golf. For Mitu, the trend and symbolism seemed pretty clear. As he'd move up the corporate ladder, his balls would become smaller.

I haven't heard too many people hailing arm wrestling, darts, chess, karate, power-lifting or many of the other competitive activities as being 'business friendly'. However, golf does figure on that list. Probably because it helps individuals discard their professional designations back in the office and interact on a level-playing field.

No one really knows if this route actually works. But if you are pushing yourself so hard for success, you might as well give yourself a break and enjoy the sport itself without wondering about what material benefits it might bring you in the future. And if hobnobbing with the corporate glitterati is all that you longed for, more power to you.

MONEY

If someone tries to sell you a get-rich-quick scheme that sounds too good to be true, it's either illegal, impractical or will end when someone pinches you in the morning. Pyramid and Ponzi schemes have been around for a long time and though they have been proved to be based on business models that are unsustainable in the long run, they surprisingly find many takers. Arbitrage opportunities (for example, a financial instrument that is priced differently across different markets), where you can make a lot of money with zero or very little risk, are far too few. The time window is too short and the tools (that is, superfast computer applications monitoring and executing deals) required to take advantage of such opportunities are too sophisticated. So you are stuck with two options – low-risk, low-returns or high-risk, high-returns. Take your pick. The options will follow. Each of the following has the potential to fall in either of those categories depending on your strategies. So tread with care.

a. Investments

In the annual reports of Berkshire Hathaway, Warren Buffet, considered by many as the God of investing, presents his company's performance to all shareholders in a fascinating style. The letter usually starts with a comparative analysis of his company versus the S&P 500. In his 2008 letter[1], he said that the compounded annual gain from 1965 to 2008 for the S&P 500 was 8.9 per cent while for Berkshire Hathaway it was 20.3 per cent. Considering that 2008 was the worst year for both in forty-four years, those returns are commendable.

This means, if you had invested in the S&P index in 1965, and forgotten all about it till 2008, your overall gain in 2008 would have been a whopping 4,276 per cent. Not bad at all, considering the 'best investor in the world' was getting 11.4 per cent more per year after putting in all those resources and effort to get that additional return, while you were just sitting there for forty-three years twiddling your thumbs.

Four decades is a long time and you may not want to wait for that long. You can decide your time horizon, but ensure that it is

[1] http://www.berkshirehathaway.com/letters/2008ltr.pdf

long enough to absorb all the boom and bust cycles (including bursting bubbles) that can skew the returns negatively.

The markets in the recent past have been battered. But if you are in it for the long haul, prudent investment in good stocks might still be an attractive investment strategy.

The high-risk, high-return version of this game is called speculation. Day traders and those with a short-term investment horizon could potentially make a killing on good days, but one bad deal could also wipe out all of that in a snap. So, we won't talk about it.

For long-term investing, whether you choose intermittent lump-sum investments or a disciplined systematic investment plan (SIP), what's more important is that your strategy and plan don't get destroyed by short-term fluctuations in the market. If you think you can't understand the complicated calculations and the financials, you could get some expert advice. But don't let your advisor blindly invest on your behalf. Ensure you understand the logic and the fundamentals before you give the green signal. Convince yourself first before you part with your hard-earned money.

But sitting for the next forty-three years, doing nothing else, will be boring. So in addition to your investment plans, you might want to take up something else that'll keep you on your feet.

b. Launch a Business

The ultimate test. This is where it all comes together – your ideas, your business plan, your contacts, your network, your team-building skills, your knowledge about every discipline (marketing, strategy, finance), your execution abilities, and most importantly, the fire in your belly. Nothing beats being in the driver's seat. It'll be your baby. It would be unwise to put yourself in a make-or-break situation. If this is the first time you are moving into this territory, keep the stakes low to begin with. Learn the ropes as you go along.

Do your homework well, before you hit the ground. Try not to push yourself to run fast when you should be crawling. Don't expect to have all the answers on day one, but also have a basic game plan in place that addresses the major areas – the concept, what makes it unique, its target market, the competition, team size, initial funding, business plan (covering the timeline, proof of concept, marketing strategy, milestones/targets), costs, the *first* customer. Rashmi Bansal's *Stay Hungry Stay Foolish* talks about successful entrepreneurs and has sold thousands of copies. This clearly highlights the interest and possible dormant potential Indians have for entrepreneurial initiatives.

The Internet is a good source of templates that you could use for your business plan. Refer to a few of them to get your own checklist in place and start filling in the gaps. Review and fine-tune it as you go along and realize areas that need more attention.

The sense of ownership will be tremendous and the learning curve will be steep. You'll have everything to gain if it works and we are not just talking about the financial upside. It's also the satisfaction of having built a successful business from scratch. You never know, business schools might start calling you to share your success stories with wide-eyed students in class.

And if it doesn't work out, well, if you've played your cards well, you'll live to see another day – a lot wiser, a lot more experienced, a lot more prepared…for that next venture.

That wraps up our whirlwind tour of options to think about. There are tons of other opportunities and this was just a teaser to get you thinking in the right direction.

For those who view the MBA as a broad-based antibiotic, hoping it would help sort out their intertwined ball of affliction, the result, more often than not, is disappointing. The potential side-effects of a powerful medication, administered casually without a thorough diagnosis, can be worse than the original problem.

A better approach would be to actually understand the specific nature of your problems and try to seek out focused solutions to address them. At best, you'll achieve your goals at a fraction of the cost and within a fraction of the timeframe. At worst, the backlash wouldn't be as severe as a failed MBA experiment and you'd still have the resources (money, energy and additional hair to be pulled out) for a second shot at the alternative options.

However, if you have analysed and understood why you need an MBA, you should push full steam ahead. Now that you are aware of the pros and cons, you'll be better equipped to face the hurdles that may come up. The pitfalls that do pop up occasionally will not be totally unexpected. And when they do, your mitigation plan will ensure that they don't sound like the death knell for your ambitions. If you have the perseverance, the patience and the potential, you will achieve what you've set your eyes on.

Of course, there's always room for improvement. But despite the seemingly ironic elements and the inherent imperfections, the whole *system* works like a well-oiled machine for B-schools that have got it right. Alumni from the good schools develop a greater appreciation for their MBA experience several years after they've bid adieu to their classmates. Their association with their alma mater continues way beyond graduation as both the school and the MBA graduate continue to reap the rewards from their mutual association. If you do your homework well and stick to one of these good schools, you will not regret your decision.

I've talked about the MBA process with an unbiased view – the good, the bad and the not-so-pleasant facets of B-school life. At the end of this book, I hope that you will embark on the MBA journey with more clarity. I hope that the book has made you an informed consumer of the MBA.

If you are the considerate type who gets emotionally attached to the characters of the book you are reading, you might've occasionally wondered what happened to our other sincere, modest friend we met in the beginning, Sachin Nimbalkar. We've given a whole lot of airtime to the flamboyant Mitu bhai, but we've let Sachin disappear. See, that's the beauty of fictional characters. You can do what you want with them and not bother about the consequences. Except, in the case of Sachin, it was intentional. Here's where we get a little philosophical, so please keep your handkerchief ready, just in case.

Sachin represents you (yes, even if you are female[2]). Sachin's story isn't over. In fact, after you put this book down, digest the contents and think of a gameplan for yourself, that's when Sachin's journey will really begin. Your choices will decide Sachin's fate and destiny. So buckle up, get your maps out, chart the best route forward and head for that destination confidently.

Good luck with your journey. It'll be a real interesting ride, that's for sure!

[2] If you are finding that difficult to relate to, mentally 'Find and Replace' Sachin with Sanchita and you'll be just fine.

Appendix A
What do the Experts Have to Say?

The objective of this book is not to break new ground in the MBA field or claim credit for the work that others have already carried out. We only want to make ourselves aware of these alternative views, so that we are equipped with the right questions to help us in our decision-making process.

The views mentioned here have been aired by people respected and revered in their fields. Much of what follows has been taken from interviews and articles.

In an article[1] entitled 'Is It Time to Retrain B-Schools?' published in the *New York Times* on 14 March 2009, Kelly Holland explored if the teaching methodology adopted by business schools had caused the most serious economic crisis in decades. Non-believers of business schools say that they have become 'too scientific, too-detached from the real-world issues', that they provide a 'limited and distorted view of their role' and that they 'graduate with a focus on maximizing shareholder value and only a limited understanding of ethical and social considerations essential to business leadership'. The article also said that some recruiters and companies questioned the value of the MBA and were telling young people that they were better off getting on-the-job training rather than heading to B-school for the same. It quoted Warren Bennis, a professor of management at the University of Southern California, as saying that the schools suffered from 'an overemphasis on the rigour and an underemphasis on relevance.'

Background Briefing, a programme hosted by Stephen Crittenden

[1] http://www.nytimes.com/2009/03/15/business/15school.html

on ABC Radio National[2] on 29 March 2009, had several important points for us to think about. The context to this was the role played by MBAs from top schools in the financial mayhem that caused the Wall Street landscape to be changed forever. The programme said that MBAs are now being called the Masters of Disasters. The views of several prominent personalities were aired in the programme. Some of these are included here along with several other sources as mentioned in the corresponding footnotes.

Henry Mintzberg, a professor of management at Canada's McGill University, is perhaps one of the most quoted and published when it comes to highlighting what's wrong with the MBA programme in specific contexts and business schools in general. His most famous quote: 'Conventional MBA programmes train the wrong people in the wrong ways with the wrong consequences.' He has written a book on the topic and it has done exceedingly well commercially. He points out that the most admired business leaders, such as Warren Buffett, Herb Kelleher, Michael Dell, Bill Gates, Jack Welch and Oprah Winfrey, do not have MBAs. He thinks[3] business schools are responsible for churning out 'trivial strategists' and dry mechanical number-crunchers rather than *thinking* managers who are able to use their judgement and use their skills judiciously. He feels there's no way that anyone can create managers in a classroom, let alone leaders. According to him, management is neither a profession nor a science – it is a practice. For him, there seems to be no doubt that the top schools are to be blamed for the recent financial meltdown, as they have been teaching a totally dysfunctional form of management practice for several years.

Another academician, Rakesh Khurana, a professor of organizational behaviour at Harvard, echoes similar sentiments in his book. He feels the practice of dangling carrots in front of managers, in the form of stock options and bonuses, to do the very jobs that they were recruited for, is counter-intuitive. In no other profession is there a need to bribe anyone with such goodies so they do their job. He feels the entire

[2] Full transcript of the programme is available on the ABC website http://www.abc.net.au/radionational/programs/backgroundbriefing/mba-mostly-bloody-awful/3143174#transcript

[3] http://www.guardian.co.uk/business/2008/apr/20/mbas.china

story started drifting in the wrong direction when maximization of shareholder interests took centre stage.[4] The company management, essentially an agent of the principal (that is, shareholders), was given mandates and powers to realize ambitious targets. Beyond maximizing profits for shareholders, companies started feeling there were no other social responsibilities. In the process, the manager stopped asking questions to evaluate if the cause was worth struggling for. In fact, whether these managers acted in the interests of their shareholders or just got carried away by self-interests in itself is another question that needs to be answered. According to the ABC Radio National interview which has highlighted Prof Khurana's views, business schools have been propagating some 'anti-social' theories which graduates go out and practise in the corporate world.

In an article[5] in the *Guardian* (UK), Gary Hamel from London Business School (LBS) is quoted as saying that business teaching often doles out so-called 'best practices' without questioning or analytically digging into the inherent concepts or the processes that it spawns. The same article also mentions concerns raised by prominent professors, including the late Sumantra Ghoshal (again from LBS), that some of the concepts taught in business schools were directly responsible for the 'corporate excesses that have discredited the past decade'.

In a paper published by the *Academy of Management Learning and Education*, Professor Pfeffer of Organizational Behaviour at the Graduate School of Business in Stanford University along with Christina Fong, said that there was very little proof that an MBA degree had much influence over salary or career. They thought the students who got in had the potential to succeed in whatever they did anyway. B-schools acted primarily as filters in selecting these high potential candidates. Another surprising factor that the authors of that paper highlighted was that MBA students were more likely to cheat than students of other disciplines.

An article[6] titled 'But can you teach it?' in *The Economist* pointed out

[4] http://business.theage.com.au/business/mba-means-little-if-its-all-business-without-management-20080527-2iqg.html

[5] http://www.guardian.co.uk/business/2008/apr/20/mbas.china

[6] http://www.cfo.com/article.cfm/3013971/1/c_2984789?f=related

that 'no form of education was more commercialized than management education', but there was uncertainty as to whether they were teaching the right things. Business schools were 'facing more criticism of the quality of their work, than they have ever done before'. Foreign students (the 'money-spinners') accounted for about 20-30 per cent in American programmes and this number was higher in European MBA programmes. The article said some of the shortcomings could be addressed by getting more corporate managers to teach in the MBA classrooms (after training them to communicate with students properly) as opposed to professional management academicians.

Phillip Delves Broughton, a former journalist with Britain's *Daily Telegraph* in Paris, took a two-year break to complete his MBA from Harvard. He also wrote about his experience in a book that has become very popular. He describes the case study approach where students are expected to read about a business situation and discuss it in class. According to Broughton, 'an enormous premium is placed on your ability to stick your hand up in front of 90 people and make a point'. He cites the response from a Chinese classmate who couldn't understand why it was important to fill air space with chatter. Back home in China, it was more important to get things done and not how good one is in meetings. Broughton also doesn't approve of the fact that getting into a prestigious school and becoming part of an elite group is considered by many as an end in itself. According to him, it is ironic to see that B-schools attract risk-averse people (unlike genuine entrepreneurs), who then go out and indulge in risky, reckless behaviour – derivatives and toxic debt being a case in point. Broughton also highlights how the oversimplification of problems hides the complexities of real life. Students spend an awful lot of time working on fancy presentations and colourful graphs which are expected to capture the essence of complicated and messy problems.

Kevin Hassett, director of economic policy studies at the American Enterprise Institute, and a Bloomberg news columnist, points the finger at two qualities that characterize MBAs – narcissism and supreme self-confidence. Speaking about the debacle on Wall Street, he says risk management was to blame as people running the show assumed that the mathematical models were foolproof.

Two Harvard professors, Srikant Datar and David Garvin, carried out detailed research to find out the state of MBA education. The methodology was quite rigorous and they included a wide cross section of people, including deans, students, recruiters, academic critics and executives. In their findings[7] they have listed many of the concerns that have been voiced earlier. Deans and recruiters do not think the phenomenon of globalization has been adapted and embraced by MBA curricula. They expect students to have a 'heightened sense of cultural awareness and a more refined global outlook'. Roughly two-thirds of all business school graduates head to consulting firms and financial service firms. However, many firms feel strong candidates who are already in these fields are better off continuing in their current roles rather than losing two years in pursuit of an MBA. Recruiters value the screening process of schools more than the degree and a few said they wouldn't mind recruiting candidates directly from the school's admission lists.

An MBA, like any other degree or academic course, has its good and bad sides. As long as you educate yourself about the pros, the cons and the pitfalls, you'll do just fine.

If the sources provided in this section encourage you to read the detailed works of these experts and help you form your own opinion, then the book would have still achieved its objective of creating well-informed readers who are better placed to address the MBA-or-not question based on their own analysis and perception.

The views expressed in this chapter reiterate the entire premise of this book. The MBA system isn't all shiny and perfect. The road to Utopia is far from smooth. It is dotted with speed-breakers. Good schools help in easing some of those road-bumps, but can't eliminate them totally. The mediocre ones could, in contrast, make these speed-bumps look like mountains. There's always the very real possibility that the common objectives – getting a good education, a great network and a decent return on investment – could all end up as wishful thinking, if you aren't careful enough.

A great school will help ensure you don't have to worry about

[7] http://hbswk.hbs.edu/item/6053.html

some of these issues. There are greater chances of the odds tilting in your favour – your knowledge will grow, you will make fantastic contacts and, in due course of time, your achievements will more than surpass your expectations. The good (but not great) schools will act as facilitators and provide you the platforms to reach your goals as well. In either case, you will have to put in considerable effort from your side.

The mediocre schools will do none of that and in your quest for a bargain MBA, you'd be lucky if you don't find yourself a few notches behind where you started from – financially and professionally.

Appendix B
A Day in the Life of an MBA Student

I wrote this while I was pursuing my degree at the Judge Business School, University of Cambridge, and it was published on the Cambridge MBA website. Though this is specific to my experience, the broad message would be more or less similar in any good business school. Compare and contrast this account with the rest of the content in this book.

6:30 a.m. The alarm goes off. Surprisingly, the intensity of my hatred towards the beeping sounds which emanate from my clock has decreased lately. And I think I know the reason for this. For the first time in eons, I'm actually doing something that I really want to do, as opposed to what clients and bosses expect me to. This in itself is a nice warm feeling, though I realize some of the warmth this morning also comes from rolling too close to the radiator.

8:00 a.m. Warm, fuzzy feelings don't last long once I start cycling in the English morning chill. My family's apartment is about fifteen minutes from Cambridge's city centre, where the Judge Business School (commonly referred to as *The Judge*) is located. The advantage of settling on the outskirts of the city is that I get a phenomenal view of the vast stretches of lush greenery that surround Cambridge. To complete the picture-perfect setting, there are even horses grazing outside the vet school, right behind our residential complex. When we first arrived, I occasionally suspected the academically charged environment was lending these horses an aura of wisdom; seeing the grandeur of King's College en route to The Judge usually dissipates those sleepy thoughts.

This morning commute is a huge change from Mumbai, where I come from. I now actually have to use my muscles to get from point A to B. Back home, I'd just have to step out of my apartment and allow the general mass of the working population to magically transport me across buses/trains to my destination in about 1.5 hours (one way). It's also strange getting used to the fact that 'personal space' here can extend beyond Mumbai's city average of, oh, 23 mm/mammal.

8:15 a.m. At The Judge, I quickly catch up on my email, sending a few quick replies and marking the rest as 'unread', hoping to tackle them over the weekend. Most classes in the Cambridge MBA expect students to do pre-reading from the core text and then usually some additional articles before class begins. For Finance & Accounting lectures today, we're expected to analyse an annual report from a publicly-traded company that deals in ready-packed produce. (Between supermarkets and fast-food outlets, that's a bigger business than you'd expect.) A few teams will present their analysis in class, which today is actually being led by the CFO of the same company! After discussing some missing pieces in our individual work, my team heads off to the lecture hall.

9:00 a.m. It's interesting to hear directly from an industry practitioner how the accounting concepts we've covered in the past couple of classes are actually applied and used in his company. As the CFO weaves theoretical concepts into a few personal anecdotes, the academics of accounting attain a more practical side. The big lesson of the day is that one-size-fits-all rules don't really exist in finance (well, maybe there are a few). Contrary to my assumptions, real-world accounting is as much an art as it is a science. Textbook financial ratios tend to get customized by companies, to better fit the way a given industry works.

12:30 a.m. Lunch-time is usually a one-and-a-half-hour 'break'. Today, I have two meetings scheduled before my next class at 2 o'clock. The first meeting is with my Study Group, to discuss how we'll tackle tomorrow's group assignment on Management Analysis (it will be timed and assessed). Each study group has five members and the MBA office makes sure each group retains most of the diversity of this international class. My group consists of an aeronautical designer (a Stanford graduate) from Boeing, a management consultant from Accenture, a lawyer and a heritage project manager. So far there hasn't been any bloodshed or violence in the group. I interpret that as meaning we're working pretty well as a team.

My second team (self-christened 'Automagic') is working on 'The Global Prize' – an extra-curricular case study competition that's organized by the consulting firm AT Kearney. Though this is a voluntary project, over 60 per cent of our class is enrolled. There's a lot of work to be done for the competition, and since my team has no formal knowledge of strategy, marketing, finance or economics, we've been tackling these domains one-by-one. Kasper, from our team, shows us some interesting Microsoft Excel tricks he's picked up during his tenure at McKinsey. Overall, the learning value from the project is enormous.

2:00 p.m. After a quick and productive brainstorming session, I'm back in the lecture room. A quick scan around the theatre reveals no bruises or black eyes on any other students. Perhaps all the sessions on interpersonal skills and team dynamics from our Management Practice course are paying off.

After bombarding the left side of my brain all morning, it's time to exercise the other half, with three hours of Marketing. Today's discussion is about Volkswagen's launch of the New Beetle in the late 90s. These interactive sessions tend to be the most entertaining classes, and it's here where varied experience and perspectives of the class really come to the forefront. In this specific instance, from the animated class debates, I learn that the Beetle was a big success in the US whereas the European markets gave it a thumbs-down sign.

5:30 p.m. Some senior representatives from a Barclays Global Investors (BGI), a financial services company, are at The Judge for an overview presentation on BGI's service/product offerings and MBA careers within the company. I attend, even though I'm not keen on moving into Finance (or so I think). For someone like me, with zero finance background, the presentation at least helps shed some light on how the industry works. By the end of the session, I'm reconsidering financial services as a potential career option.

7:30 p.m. I had sent across my first CV to the Careers Service for their review during orientation, *before* the MBA programme had officially started. I was expecting an action-packed year ahead of me, but it still started earlier than I expected.

Along with the corporate interaction organized by the Judge Business School, the Careers Service at the University of Cambridge also organizes many events, though most are geared to undergraduates. But MBA students can tag along for any event that sounds interesting. This evening, there's a reception organized by The Boston Consulting Group at the Crowne Plaza Hotel, just across the street. So I dash off to the hotel, chat with a few consultants and get their version of 'a day-in-the-life'.

9:00 p.m. Back home, I have dinner with Alisha (my two-year-old daughter) and Swati (my wife – her exact age is still a mystery to me). I practise some of my recently acquired skills by explaining to Alisha why her good friends Pooh Bear and Barney might not get along in business together, due to inherent mismatches in their personality types. I draw up some elaborate 2-by-2 matrices comparing and contrasting individual traits to organization types, backed up with some psychological profiling techniques, and, for the record, I can state that I get no counter-questions from her.

10:00 p.m. After attending the company reception in the evening, I work on a cover letter for my CV and send it across. Some more pre-reading for tomorrow's Organization Behaviour class, and then I get to crash for the day.

* * *

If you ask other students from the Cambridge MBA, I'm sure their 'day-in-the-life' stories for today might sound quite different from mine

(I'd expect a few overlaps, hopefully). For example, lots of students stay in college accommodation, which adds a whole new dimension to the social life in Cambridge.

It's not a stretch, I think, to compare the Cambridge MBA (or any other leading one-year programme) to a massive, multi-course meal. You can take what appeals to your own personal tastes, or your appetite. More often than not, there are tough choices between various options that you might like, but don't have time for. In our Finance class, we learnt the concept of time-value of money wherein future cash-flows have diminishing value. Makes you wonder why these universal concepts don't apply to time itself. In other words, shouldn't the clock have more hours now than it did when life was presumably simpler?

On that (ahem!) pseudo-intellectual thought, allow me to sign off.

Appendix C
Useful links

No single book (apart from a telephone directory) can claim to comprehensively include 100 per cent of the information related to a particular topic. Whether it's plain modesty or commercial naivete, we've admitted at the outset that this book does not claim to provide 100 per cent authentic or credible information on every single aspect that it touches upon.

Apart from the irrational little red devil (residing in my mind), responsible for most of the paranoid thoughts expressed here, several other information sources have been referenced while working on this book. Some of these are listed below. If any of the links have been updated, just go to the homepage of these sites and navigate down to the relevant sections. Make Google your best friend in your quest for the *real* story out there.

BUSINESSWEEK

Contains a good collection of articles related to business schools. Make sure you check out the MBA diaries, where representatives from the top B-schools across the world share their stories from admissions to graduation.

I was a big fan of the BW discussion forum (http://forums.businessweek.com/). Almost everything that's directly or indirectly related to B-schools has been covered here. I loved it because it had a huge number of uncertain, scared and paranoid souls like me asking intelligent, relevant and at times downright stupid questions.

About.com

If you are just starting out then the Business Majors sub-site (http://businessmajors.about.com/) on About.com provides a good introduction to the MBA game. It covers the basics – admissions, interviews, recommendations, grants/scholarships, careers, internships, etc. – but isn't too detailed. After you've gained a basic idea of what to expect in the MBA journey, you may want to move on to other sources of information.

Rankings

Some of the popular rankings that focus predominantly on US B-schools:

Business Week (http://www.businessweek.com/bschools/)

Forbes (http://www.forbes.com/)

US News (http://grad-schools.usnews.rankingsandreviews.com/best-graduate-schools/top-business-schools)

Fortune and *The Wall Street Journal* also publish B-school rankings. A few other sites that publish global rankings are listed below:

The Economist (http://mba.eiu.com/)
Financial Times (http://rankings.ft.com/rankings/mba/rankings.html)

As is the case with all rankings, do not take these at face value. Try to dig a little deeper and check out the parameters and the methodology behind these lists. Do they incorporate elements that are important from *your* perspective? Apart from the key lists mentioned here, there are several others as well. Despite the lack of a standardized approach to rankings, schools realize their importance and the critical role they play in establishing or destroying reputations.

MIT OpenCourseWare

If you want to limit your financial investment in management education to your monthly broadband connection charges, here is a fantastic alternative.

MIT, one of the most respected names in the scholastic circle, has opened up its academic treasure chest and allowed the general public access to its courseware (http://ocw.mit.edu/OcwWeb/Sloan-School-of-Management/)

Apart from covering the basics of any regular MBA programme such as Operations Management, Financial Accounting, Business Strategy, Supply Chain Planning, Information Technology, Analysing Financial Statements, Investments, Marketing, Systems Optimization, Entrepreneurship, Psychology, Linear Programming, Economic Analysis, they also have several unconventional and highly specialized courses. Some examples – Real Estate Economics, Global Climate Change Policy, Advanced Stochastic Processes, Literature, Ethics and Authority, Digital Anthropology.

If any of these topics sounds interesting, it is worth visiting the website to download the course material and check out the details. It may also give you a taste of what to expect when you are actually sitting in an MBA class.

The Personal MBA

This is an innovative programme (http://personalmba.com/) to gain the MBA knowledge without having to leave the comfort of your home. The foundation for this programme is a list of around seventy books that will cost you roughly 60,000 rupees. The website probably considers the pricing for the international editions of these books. If you can get your hands on the Indian editions, the cost falls dramatically. The candidate takes on a self-paced journey and is assisted by the virtual classroom in the form of discussion forums and coaching. Interesting concept, if you don't expect top companies to line up at your doorstep after you finish the course. A good option if you are looking for an education rather than a degree.

Vault

The site (http://vault.com) has career-related information. It covers most of the conventional and some unconventional post-MBA career options. It includes industry profiles, company profiles, employee surveys, salary surveys, resume writing tips, handling interviews. The website also features discussion forums where candidates discuss general and specific topics related to industries and companies.

Vault.com also publishes a series of industry-specific guides that have an in-depth coverage of the career options, roles and designations, what to expect in the recruitment phase, skills needed to survive in the industry, exit options and many related topics.

WETFEET

Like Vault, this site (http://www.wetfeet.com/) also focuses on careers. It was founded by two MBAs from Stanford who were looking for resources they could use in their own career searches. They couldn't find what they were looking for and decided to start creating the tools and information on their own. Their *Insider Guides* offer a peek into several career options and industries. They are particularly popular among MBA candidates.

PAGALGUY.COM

This is the biggest MBA platform in India. According to a survey, it gets 90 per cent of all MBA-related queries from India. Though you'll find a lot of GMAT and international B-school-related discussions on the discussion forums, it pales in comparison to the attention showered by applicants on CAT, IIMs and the plethora of other MBA programmes available within India. The number of registered users (several lakhs and growing) on the site can give any international MBA site a run for their money. Allwin Agnel, the founder, launched the site before his MBA, went on sabbatical to Wharton (for his MBA) while his trusted lieutenants, Apurv Pandit and Rohit Awasthi, held fort. IIM, Bangalore has a case study on this success story. If you are a budding entrepreneur, read up on their interesting and inspiring story.

PUBLICATIONS

Managers Not MBAs, A Hard Look at the Soft Practice of Managing and Management Development, Henry Mintzberg (Berrett-Koehler).

The End of Business Schools? Less Success Than Meets the Eye: Research Paper by Jeffrey Pfeffer and Christina Fong (Graduate School of Business, Stanford), www.aomonline.org.

From Higher Aims to Hired Hands: The Social Transformation of American Business Schools and the Unfulfilled Promise of Management as a Profession by Rakesh Khurana, Princeton University Press.

Business Schools Share the Blame for Enron by Sumantra Ghoshal (*Financial Times*, 17 July 2003).

Any important omissions from this list are totally unintentional. If you come across any good sites that would be useful to readers of this book, do let me know.

ENTRANCE EXAMS

GMAT

This is the official site (http://www.mba.com/mba/thegmat) for the test and addresses most topics related to it. As the concept of a computer adaptive test[1] may be new to most first-timers (specially those who have initially worked with paper-based standardized tests), it helps to be well aware of how the process works. It explains the structure (format and timing) of the test, allows free test preparation software, a list of test centres, schools that accept GMAT scores. It also provides tips for D-Day. You can schedule an appointment through the site when you are ready to take the test. The general advice here is to spend three to six months preparing for the test.

You might also want to check out the two leading test preparation options: *The Princeton Review* and *Kaplan*. They provide classes, books, CDs with examples and full-length practice tests. According to chat forums and sites like GMAT Tutor (http://www.gmattutor.com/

---

[1] A format in which the computer adjusts the difficulty level of questions depending on how the candidate has performed in previous questions. The candidate is provided only one question at a time. Starting with medium complexity, for every correct answer that the candidate provides, the subsequent questions get relatively tougher and vice versa.

book3.html) and About.com (http://businessmajors.about.com/od/satgmatpreparation/tp/gmatprepbooks.htm), *The Princeton Review* method provides strategies and short cuts for scoring high on the test, whereas *Kaplan* provides a structured step-by-step approach. *Kaplan* tests are considered harder than the actual exams whereas *The Princeton Review*'s tests are relatively easier. Pick up both books at the book store and judge for yourself. There's also the *Official Guide for GMAT Review* (go for the latest edition) by Educational Testing Services.

For most Indian applicants (many are engineers and comfortable with the quantitative part), the verbal section proves to be the Achilles' heel when it comes to cracking the GMAT. If that's your story too, a little help from a verbal-focussed course might help. For instance, you could check out CrackVerbal, a Bangalore-based GMAT training venture founded by Arun Jagannathan, a well-respected name in the test prepration industry. Taking the verbal section score a few notches higher can do wonders for the overall GMAT score as well.

TOEFL

Like its GMAT counterpart, this site (www.toefl.org) talks about the whys, the whats, the hows and the wheres of this test. Usually candidates get so psyched up about the more difficult GMAT test that the TOEFL, in comparison, is not considered to be a major hurdle to cross. But never underestimate the power of Murphy's Laws.

What I've listed here is just the tip of the iceberg. When it comes to seeking information from published sources, be aware that editing and censorship could get in the way and make it difficult for you to get the complete picture. So, I'd strongly recommend that you expand your information sources to include people who have gone through the process or know someone else who has. Depending on the articulation skills, the level of trust and the emotional intensity of your contact, the information sharing will be richer and far more colourful than any other source.

Appendix D
The Query List

I know, I know. This book has given you more questions than answers and the last thing you'd expect from the appendix is more of the same. But that is exactly the intention – to get you to ask more questions and find out the answers that apply to your situation rather than be content with the standard one-size-fits-all solutions.

So here's a long list of questions to ask yourself at various stages of your journey. Consider this as a way to wrap up most of what we discussed in the other chapters. You could use this list as a starting point and add your own queries to it. Don't fret too much about questions that do not apply to you. Just move on to the next one.

Let's first address the notion of a 'good' school that we've been harping about in this book. What is a good school anyway?

A list of schools that you could blindly pick up and start applying to would've been excellent to have. It would save everyone a whole lot of time and effort. It would allow one to jump right into the intimidating process of applications. Unfortunately, there is no absolute answer to that million dollar question.

I frequently get asked by MBA hopefuls, 'What's a good GMAT score?' My answer usually is, 'Any score that gets you into the school of your choice is good.' Those expecting to hear a magic number in response aren't too happy on hearing my reply. A score of 780 doesn't automatically get the top schools laying out the red carpet for you. Similarly, a score of 650 won't necessarily make them close their doors for you, even if their median or average scores are higher.

My response to the question about 'good schools' echoes similar sentiments. The term *good* is relative. What's good for me may not be good for you. The top ten or even the top hundred schools in popular rankings may not be good from your perspective, if they don't address your concerns. You'll have to define a list of criteria that's important for you to meet *your* goals. Then draw up a list of schools that meet most or all of the criteria. And you'll get your list of good schools. The process is not as simple as one would have desired, but that's how it is. The maxim – Act in haste and repent at leisure – is very true when it comes to B-schools.

For the sake of illustration, consider schools like Harvard, Stanford, Wharton, MIT (Sloan), Haas (Anderson), Virginia (Darden) or any of the other top ten American business schools that offer two-year MBA programmes. For a lot of people, these would be great schools, considering the brand power, the fantastic quality of people you would be studying with and the amazing professors that you would learn from. But the cost of attending these schools is so prohibitively high that they move out of many applicants' shortlists despite being great (not just good) programmes.

Use the questions provided below to start the process. It's going to be a while till you get the answers to most of these questions. But at the end of it, you will hopefully have a less-cluttered perspective and that should give you more clarity on the future direction.

INTROSPECTION

- Where am I right now in my profession? In my personal life?
- If I continue to go with the flow, where will I end up in the next five to ten years?
- What do I like about my current job and what do I hate?
- Is any of this really a problem or is it just my mind exaggerating things out of proportion?
- Is my current job something I see myself doing for the next ten years? Twenty years?
- What are the hobbies that I really enjoy? Is it practically and financially feasible to take up anything related to these as a part-time or full-time profession?

- What do I really want? More money, a career change, intellectual stimulation, a promotion, a change of cities/countries, new skills, new qualifications?
- Have I seriously explored all the other alternatives that can help me reach where I want to be?
- Why have I discarded each of these options?
- If each of the options individually can't help my cause, can I consider a combination that'll work for me?
- What's my current financial position?
- Am I depending only on a single source of income? Do I have supplementary sources of income (such as investments in stocks)?
- What are the implications if my primary source of income stops for a couple of years?
- Do I have any other important financial investments (house, marriage, children's education, alimony) coming up in the next few years?
- Am I simply facing burnout? Will a nice long vacation help me rejuvenate and hit the road again?
- Why do I want to pursue an MBA? How will it help me get what I want?

Pre-Admission

- Is a full-time MBA programme the only way to reach my goals? Can I consider other options – part-time MBA, correspondence MBA, executive MBA?
- Is it too early or too late for me to make such an investment?
- Do I have the basic experience in management or leadership to wring out the best from my investment?
- What kind of MBA programmes should I look at?
- Are rankings for the school important for what I'm trying to achieve?
- Would I like to be part of a big class or would I prefer smaller MBA programmes?
- In which country do I want to work after the MBA?

- If I am not a citizen of that country, how easy or difficult would it be for me to get a work permit?
- Should I look at MBA programmes outside the country?
- When do I intend to start the programme?
- Do I have enough time to take care of all the pre-requisites – the entrance tests, the applications, the interviews, loans, visa formalities – before the programme starts?
- Do I have a well-thought-out schedule in place for each part of the application phase?
- How much time should I spend on preparing for GMAT?
- Should I chalk out a self-study plan or should I join a class?
- Have I talked to enough number of people who have gone through the process?
- Did they have backgrounds similar to mine? Did their objectives differ from mine?
- What are they doing currently and how did they get there? Did they consider other (non-MBA) options as well?
- Based on all the inputs and my own analysis, do I have a shortlist of schools that I would apply to? Does it have a good combination of dream schools and safe bets?
- What's the placement track record of these schools when it comes to placing students in the area of my interest?
- What role does the careers' team play in the process? Are they proactive or do they perform a supporting role while students fend for themselves?
- Do these schools have rolling admissions or discrete rounds?
- Am I hoping to get some financial aid or scholarships from these schools or from other organizations?
- Can I tap into external sources for financial assistance?

ADMISSIONS

- Have I contacted alumni from my shortlisted schools? What do they have to say about the schools that hasn't already been mentioned on the official websites?
- Do they have any tips for me in terms of the application process, the interview, the career hunt (considering my objectives)?

- Am I targeting the first rounds of admissions or it really doesn't matter?
- Have I thoroughly thought through the essay questions in the applications?
- Has the essay writing process provided me with insights about myself that I hadn't previously thought about?
- Do I have a fairly good idea of what the school is looking for in prospective students? Where do I place myself on their grading curve?
- Have I got my essays proof-checked, reviewed critically (embedded question: Do I need an external consultant?) and ensured that the word-count limits are adhered to?
- From a third party's perspective, what kind of an image do these essays portray? Is this what I had in mind when I started writing them?
- Are there key points which I assumed people would read in, but which have not been clearly highlighted?
- Do I have solid evidence (documents, certificates, references, convincing details to my stories) to back up my claims?
- How are interviews conducted? On-campus, on the phone, by alumni?
- Is there a standard structure that gets followed in the interview and is there anything I can do specifically to prepare for it?
- Does the school have a tie-up with banks for student loans? Will they help facilitate the application process?
- Would the loan cover 100 per cent of the tuition? Will it also cover living expenses?
- What are the interest rates? What is the moratorium period offered by this institution; that is, when do I start the repayments (usually it is six months after graduation)?
- Can I locate other sources that provide funding with better terms and conditions?
- If my post-MBA income is in a different currency (vis-à-vis the student-loan currency), will I be exposing myself to foreign exchange-rate fluctuations during the repayment period? If so, is there a way to hedge this risk?

- Will I need to dip into my own savings to bridge the funding gap?
- How will my dependents (if any) be impacted by the altered cash flow status?
- Do I have to arrange for accommodation on my own or will the school help me with this?
- Will I have to live in university premises? Can I take a look at the rooms before signing up?
- If the school's definition of a 'modest student accommodation' is a four-feet-by-six-feet dingy rat-infested storehouse, can I explore options outside as well?
- Are there private accommodation options available? Are they worth the additional premium I'm being asked to shell out?
- What will I do for food? Are there cooking facilities available if I'm tired of ordering pizzas and takeaways?
- What other basic necessities will I need to carry with me, that aren't already provided by the university?
- Can I get the basic syllabus from the school in advance?
- Have I been able to identify the areas where I'll have to work harder because I have no background in that area (statistics, basic excel modelling skills, etc.)?
- Can I do some pre-reading before I land up in the school campus, so I can hit the ground running when the course starts?
- Will I have to buy a new laptop or will the school arrange for one? What are the compatibility requirements for the schools network?
- Do I have the basic software (for example, MS Office) installed on the laptop? Is my anti-virus software updated? Am I carrying the original CDs with me just in case my laptop crashes during the course and I have to reformat it and start from scratch?

MBA

- (On the first day in class) – Who are all these strange-looking characters around me and why can't I picture any of them on the cover of *Fortune* magazine anytime soon? Where are all the hot, smouldering ones that usually figure on the B-school brochure?

- Have I had a chance to at least browse through all the pre-reading material that was handed over by the school when we arrived?
- How does the schedule for the week look? Do I have a plan to tackle the workload?
- While I'm slogging my ass away just to keep pace with the day-to-day expectations, why does everyone around me look and sound so confident?
- Do I need to start initiating the efforts on the career front?
- Am I developing a deeper interest or dislike in specific areas?
- Do I have a list of electives for the year? Are there any that I definitely want to take up?

Internship

- How does the internship process work in this school?
- Is there flexibility in terms of the internship duration? How long and how short can it be?
- Have any companies already approached the school and provided a list of projects that they'd like to carry out?
- Will I have to compete with others within my class for this internship?
- Can I apply for one or more of these opportunities? Is there a bidding process?
- Will it be a paid internship? Will they reimburse out-of-pocket expenses (travel, food etc.)?
- Will the internship involve travel and meeting people? Or is it an independent-research type of project that I can execute using B-school resources (space, databases, network, internet, faculty assistance)?
- Will I have a mentor from the sponsoring organization? What will their role be during the process?
- Are the deliverables and the milestones clearly defined for the internship?

- Will the sponsoring organization be open to considering your suggestion for expanding, reducing or altering the scope of work?
- How will your efforts be judged? How will the organization define the success or failure of the project?
- Will you get a chance to interact with other people within the organization who are not directly concerned with the internship?
- Will you be able to find out about all the other areas that the sponsoring organization is involved in? From a longer-term career perspective, would any of those businesses be of more interest than your current focus area?
- Do you get the opportunity to explore the culture of the organization? Would you be comfortable working in this type of environment?
- Are there alumni from your school working in this organization? Were they also interns here before taking up full-time positions?
- What is the likelihood of interns in this organization being offered permanent positions?

Networking

- What kind of networking options does the school provide? How many of these would be of direct interest to me?
- Are there any special interest groups that I could join? What are their activities and are they really going to be worth the time and possibly, money, I spend on them?
- Are there any conferences or seminars or panel discussions coming up that sound interesting? What do I have to do to get on the invitee list?
- Will there be an informal session for networking after the formal event?
- Can I initiate anything on my own to supplement the networking options presented by the school?
- Can I access the alumni database to find out contacts in the company, the country and the industry of my interest?

- Will they be open to informational interviews over the phone or in person?
- Do I have a list of relevant questions ready for the meeting?

CAREER

- Do I have a list of criteria ready to shortlist companies that I could approach?
- Are the companies recruiting? If not, why not? Is the situation expected to change over the coming months?
- Do these companies have a presence on campus?
- Do they organize various events to establish a relationship with the new cohort?
- How can I ensure I attend as many of them as possible (if not all)? How else can I get onto their radar (in a positive way, of course)?
- When do they start the actual recruiting process?
- Is there a specific position that they are trying to fill in or is this part of their generic recruitment process?
- What are the various stages in their recruiting process?
- Do these include technical interviews, personality-based questions, case studies, quantitative problems?
- Can you have mock sessions for each of them using the help of the careers' team or fellow classmates?
- What happens after an offer is made? When is the candidate expected to join?
- Is it a rotational role? Would I be expected to work in various departments before being placed in one?
- Do they have offices outside the country? Can they consider me for overseas placements?
- Will they help out with work permit applications, if required?
- How is their salary structured? What do the fixed and variable components include? How are bonuses calculated?
- What's the total 'take-home' salary that I'll get after making all deductions (for example, taxes)?
- With this salary, how many years will it take me to repay my loan?

Next Steps

You could have continued to do what most others interested in an MBA will continue to do. You could have taken the plunge into the turbulent waters without knowing what to expect. But you did not let that happen. You decided to complete reading the book, hoping to stumble upon some gems that you could actually use for yourself. And hopefully, you did.

By now, you have thought well through the process. You've done your homework and carried out your own research to supplement and validated the data compiled by prominent publications. You have a practical and well-balanced view of what the MBA can and cannot do for you. You have done enough introspection to evaluate if this is what you want to do at this stage of your career. You are aware of the common practices within the industry. You know what to expect within and outside the classroom. You know the good schools from the mediocre ones. You have not allowed rankings to blindly influence your decision while shortlisting schools.

In short, you are now a serious contender for the top B-schools. In the next appendix, we'll cover specifics of how you can improve your chances of getting into the best MBA programmes and increase the odds of professional success.

Appendix E
How to Get into the Best MBA Programmes

In the earlier chapters, we've covered a whole lot of ground about the pros and cons of taking up the MBA route to reach your career goals. Once you have done the basic introspection and are convinced that a good MBA degree can work wonders for your career, the next step in the process is to create a personalized MBA application strategy that will improve your odds of getting into the best possible school for you.

In this appendix, let's cover the basics of what you need to do for each part of the MBA application – starting from understanding your strengths and weaknesses to executing a well-crafted action plan to perfection.

HOW TO MAKE YOUR PROFILE IRRESISTIBLE TO THE TOP SCHOOLS

'*I plan to apply to the top business schools in two to three years. What can I do during this period to build my profile for the best MBA programmes?*'

This is another of those frequently asked questions (FAQs) that I come across on various discussion threads that I am active on. Typically the question comes from *freshers,* that is, folks who have just graduated from engineering (BE), BCom, BSc and other streams. But many students who haven't even completed their basic graduation are also anxious to know how to make their profile irresistible to many of their dream schools.

The simple answer I could give you is that there's no such magic formula to aim for. But let's look at some factors you can still focus on to improve your chances of getting into the best B-schools.

Earlier in this book there was a section that focused on how four specific 'soft' skills can get you into the top schools. This time we are talking about the 'hard' skills. Parameters that you can put your finger on. Things you'll be able to pick up in a regular firm if you are committed and diligent.

1. Choose an Under-represented Industry or Role

It's not that the Information Technology (IT) industry is inferior in any way. Far from it. In fact, the salary, perks, opportunities in the IT industry are far better than in many other conventional industries.

But the problem is there are far too many aspirants applying from this field. And the mainstream roles (such as software development, testing /quality assurance, business analysis, project management) also won't get you that '*Oh, is that what you do?*' kind of an awe-inspiring reaction.

So if you have the opportunity, choose an industry that you love (very important, but tough to decide when you've never worked before) and possibly one that you would want to continue in, even after completing your MBA.

2. Be Part of an Exclusive Club

Once you've chosen your target industry, aim for the market leaders in the field if you can. For instance, a huge number of consultants who get into Harvard, Stanford or Wharton have already worked for McKinsey, Bain or Boston Consulting Group. Each industry has its list of companies with a halo around them. Within technology you have Google, Facebook, Amazon (Retail? Technology? Take your pick), IBM.

If the company you work for has a very competitive and tough recruiting process, it gives the admission committee the feeling that you are the cream-of-the-cream in your chosen industry.

3. Take on Responsibilities That Your Peers Can't or Won't

Most of your colleagues at work would complain about getting overloaded with responsibilities. Evaluate your situation differently. If you are doing the exact same thing five days a week and twelve hours a day, you aren't making much progress in terms of getting an exposure to new aspects of the business.

Create new learning curves for yourself. Apart from the technical skills you are picking up, keep an eye out for opportunities that need business skills.

See if you can volunteer for special projects that have a strategic importance for the management.

4. Have a Life Outside Work

Even if you are the most brilliant professional in your company and your bosses think you are the next best thing after sliced bread, your MBA classmates may not agree. You don't want to be the unidimensional professional nerd in the study group.

At work, your roles and responsibilities are more stringently defined. Outside work, you are the king of your universe. Rather than while away the free time, see if you can use it productively.

Play a sport that you like, join a social cause early on in your career, start a small entrepreneurial venture on the side. Experiment with many things in the earlier days and then focus on a few that truly excite you. By the time you are ready to apply, you'd be amazed at how much you've been able to achieve in your spare time.

5. Show EQ as well as IQ

Well, this isn't exactly a hard skill. But your Emotional Quotient (EQ) is a good glue to bind the earlier four points.

Whether you are at work or play, nobody likes a jerk. A high IQ without a high EQ would push you into Jerk-land (and no, that doesn't put you in an exclusive club).

While you are working on the top four aspects, show some maturity, professionalism, modesty and other attributes that separate the good human being from the rest.

There you go. These were the five 'secret' ingredients to make your profile irresistible to the best MBA programmes at the top B-schools. We've left out factors like a high GMAT score (most Indians score high anyway), excellent academic grades (not much you can do if you've already messed this up) and mother's blessings (which you'd hopefully be able to manage after a short sentimental discussion).

But what if you've never worked with a market leader, and never been exposed to the post-MBA industry you want to work in, and never done anything that your peers haven't?

In this case it might be a good idea to spread out the risk of applying. Choose a mix of schools that go across Ambitious, Stretch and Practical categories. Then create an application strategy (including a solid storyline) that presents your profile in the best possible manner.

With the right preparation and the right perspectives, you can manage this on your own. Each subsequent appendix should give you a headstart to manage the individual 'streams' that form the bigger MBA application.

Appendix F
How to Choose the Right Country for Your MBA

An MBA from America isn't the same as an MBA from, say, the UK or India or any other country. So how do you decide on the country? For starters, become familiar with the visa regulations within the country. Are they student-friendly or do they expect you to get a degree and return back to your home country? If getting back to India is anyway on your road map, what kind of jobs will you get after returning? Will the international MBA brand be equally valued in India?

The UK used to have something called as a Highly Skilled Migrant Programme (HSMP) that made it easy for international students to get a work permit. The precondition was that that the MBA student should have graduated from any of the top fifty B-schools in the world. The HSMP website had a list of these top B-schools. Recently, there has been a significant overhaul of the work visa process. That has been a cause of concern for many international students. However, the top MBA programmes in the UK have published encouraging placement statistics. For instance, the Cambridge MBA had a 97 per cent placement record.

In Canada, graduating from a B-school like Ivey offers something special for international MBA candidates that many of the top schools in the US and Europe don't have – the Post-graduation Work Permit Programme. This allows MBA students to convert their study visa into a work permit immediately after completing their programme. This allows them an additional one year to stay back in Canada. Graduating from Rotman, another Canadian B-school, gives you three extra years to find your foothold in the domestic job market. That's a huge psychological advantage.

American B-schools attract the maximum number of international students. If you are planning to study in the US on an F1 visa, you should be aware of the Optional Practical Training (OPT). Under this, MBA students on an F1 visa are authorized to work in the US for a period of up to twelve months while studying or on completion of the course. The employment must be directly related to the student's major area of study. So, candidates have time to get their work permits (H-1B visas) and need not start worrying about it immediately upon completion of their MBA.

However, don't assume that the visa regulations alone will open or close the doors to career opportunities within that country. If you can convince a recruiter that your skills will be useful to them, they will manage the visa application for you.

How Does an Economic Downturn Impact School Admissions?

The last few years haven't been kind. Most good and capable professionals in enviable pre-MBA jobs that offered exciting career prospects and high salaries had to face the heat of an economy that went spiralling out of control, in the wrong direction. Companies felt that the easiest way to deal with it was to cut costs, and employees were easy targets. So much for the 'Our-employees-are-our-biggest-assets' spiel.

Interestingly, in an economic downturn, B-schools get more applications than in a normal economy. Here's why. During a recession, many professionals lose their jobs for reasons that are beyond their control. Rather than staying out of work and waiting for the economy to recover, many feel that this may be a good time to go back to school and pick up a few new skills and reinvent their stagnating career graphs. They hope that the new degree, along with the retraining, will help them get back into the corporate world and accelerate their professional journey.

This is precisely what happened in the last few years. A whole lot of guys who got the short end of the stick didn't know how to deal with the unexpected change of events. Many started looking at MBA programmes to fill in the vacuum. But the B-school application process isn't easy or fast. It takes at least one full year for applicants to go through the whole rigmarole of GMAT preparation, TOEFL/IELTS test, MBA essay writing, recommendation, transcripts, etc.

And then, if you haven't got another job in the interim, there's the difficult part of explaining what you did in the previous one year before joining B-school. Dealing with lay-offs (redundancies) and forced career breaks can be a tricky aspect to manage in B-school applications.

How Do You Handle that Situation?

One good way to tackle career breaks is to talk about how you converted the forced break into a sabbatical—whether you went on a backpacking tour, or learnt to play the piano, or got trained in a new language or volunteered for some cause that you believe in. Use that to explain how you grew on the personal front when you were suddenly blessed with a lot of free time and complete freedom to pursue activities outside work.

The regular professional life saps the energy out of employees and that's one of the big excuses applicants have for not having any time for pursuing activities that interest them.

Use your essays to demonstrate how you saw opportunity in adversity. You could have slid into depression and sat in a corner sulking. But you didn't do that. That demonstrates your maturity and your perseverance. Businesses and people both go through bad phases. If you've managed to resurrect yourself from personal crises, chances are you'll be able to use that trait to do the same for the businesses that you lead after the MBA.

Appendix G
How to Select the Right B-school

Here's a simple (?) process you can follow:

Step 1: For those who are just starting out, a good launch pad would be to check out the MBA rankings for the best business schools (in *Financial Times, BusinessWeek* et al.).

Apart from the B-school's position, most of these rankings also include several other useful parameters related to entry criteria and placement statistics.

But these listings are too big to bite your teeth into. So there has to be a way to narrow it down.

Step 2: Build up a list of parameters that are important to you, such as the geography (country/city), duration of the programme (two years vs one year), career goals, target companies (check out which B-schools they frequently recruit from), class size (small intimate environment vs big classes), average age, average GMAT score, brand power.

Using your custom-built framework, you can quickly eliminate many of the names from the MBA ranking list and bring it down to a manageable number.

Step 3: This is where you keep the rankings aside and move to the official websites of the B-schools to find out details that weren't included in the standard rankings – such as school culture, electives offered, school strengths, industry connections. Hopefully you'll eliminate a few more names from your list.

Step 4: MBA forums such as the GMAT Club, Beat the GMAT, Pagalguy and MBA Crystal Ball will have a number of discussions happening around the B-schools you are interested in. Join in and post your questions. The current students and alumni active on the forum will be able to share their thoughts. Some of this can be useful, some can be confusing. So be prepared to tackle the information overload.

Step 5: Now that you have done your online research, you're in a better position to talk to current students, alumni and admission officers in an offline manner. The interactions will be more structured and productive.

Of course, all this will not happen overnight. So you need to spend a significant amount of time and effort to create a list of B-schools of your interest.

Simulation options such as the MBA Mock Application Process (MBA MAP), described later in the book, can be useful in speeding up the process. But it won't completely eliminate your independent efforts.

WHICH ARE THE MOST POPULAR B-SCHOOLS IN THE WORLD?

At MBA Crystal Ball we did a little experiment. Instead of focussing on MBA rankings (there are too many of them already), we thought of trying to look at B-schools from a popularity perspective.

We weren't interested in presenting old wine in a new bottle. Instead, we tried to create new wine and present it in a familiar-looking bottle (that is, the rankings format).

The MBA Crystal Ball B-school Ranking is not about the biggest or the best business schools in the world (based on quality of teaching or diversity of the class profile). It's also not about the highest post-MBA salaries, the average GMAT scores or, for that matter, anything related to the specific degrees (MBA, MPhil, MFE, PhD) they award. Those questions have already been addressed by others (*Financial Times, BusinessWeek, US News* et al.).

METHODOLOGY FOR THE MBA CRYSTAL BALL B-SCHOOL RANKINGS

For the scope of this B-school ranking, we restrict the definition of 'popularity' to the interest shown by prospective students, employers, professors, and other stakeholders in the online 'properties' of the B-school, primarily its website and its social media presence (limited for now to Facebook, Twitter and LinkedIn).

The B-school rankings methodology we follow is quite simple. Like in a democratic election, we've assumed that people have already voted for the most popular B-schools. We've just tapped into the publicly available data to form a perception about the level of popular interest in these business schools.

Which means: no surveys, no questionnaires, no subjective or philosophical questions to answer and no sample size constraints. Instead of limiting ourselves to a few thousand participants, we are relying upon the collective wisdom and interest of hundreds of thousands of folks who have voted with their mouse clicks.

We consider aspects such as the overall website traffic and multiple parameters (followers, likes, interactions, online activity) that are relevant for the individual social media sites. We then use a little magic formula (consisting of weights, adjustments and penalties) to arrive at the overall B-school ranks.

You'll have the names of several good schools in this ranking. Look at it as the starting point and dig deeper to find out which school fits your profile and your post-MBA goals.

MOST POPULAR BUSINESS SCHOOLS IN THE WORLD

Rank	Business School Name	Country	Website Rank	Facebook Rank	Twitter Rank	LinkedIn Rank
1	Harvard Business School	USA	25	1	3	2
2	Stanford Univ. GSB	USA	2	7	1	14
3	IMD Switzerland	Switzerland	45	4	34	1
4	Hong Kong UST (HKUST)	China	30	2	44	22
5	IE Business School	Spain	29	6	4	4
6	Univ. of Virginia – Darden	USA	18	3	8	7

Rank	Business School Name	Country	Website Rank	Facebook Rank	Twitter Rank	LinkedIn Rank
7	Univ. of Pennsylvania – Wharton	USA	8	8	2	9
8	London Business School	UK	36	5	53	5
9	MIT Sloan School of Management	USA	1	12	5	12
10	Univ. of California at Berkeley – Haas	USA	3	11	6	23
11	Vanderbilt Univ. – Owen	USA	26	49	39	3
12	City Univ. – Cass London	UK	38	10	10	25
13	Columbia Business School	USA	7	16	22	21
14	Univ. of Texas at Austin – McCombs	USA	4	33	7	36
15	Northwestern Univ. – Kellogg	USA	21	13	25	15
16	INSEAD France / Singapore	France	34	39	23	6
17	Cornell Univ. – Johnson	USA	5	35	25	13
18	Rotterdam School of Management	Netherlands	48	9	21	24
19	New York Univ. – Stern	USA	11	29	14	19
20	Duke Univ. – Fuqua	USA	22	14	12	41
21	Univ. of Michigan – Ross	USA	6	23	24	29

Rank	Business School Name	Country	Website Rank	Facebook Rank	Twitter Rank	LinkedIn Rank
22	Yale School of Management	USA	12	19	13	40
23	Indian School of Business (ISB)	India	32	20	16	16
24	SDA Bocconi	Italy	47	24	9	17
25	IESE Business School	Spain	33	34	30	8
26	Wisconsin School of Business	USA	8	52	49	10
27	Univ. of Cambridge – Judge	UK	14	18	28	32
28	Univ. of Southern California – Marshall	USA	17	17	37	28
29	Univ. of Oxford – Saïd	UK	16	31	11	39
30	Warwick Business School	UK	44	15	20	31
31	Univ. of Chicago – Booth	USA	37	37	17	18
32	UCLA – Anderson	USA	10	38	46	27
33	York Univ. – Schulich	Canada	24	32	15	35
34	Esade Business School	Spain	35	40	45	11
35	Indiana Univ. – Kelley	USA	20	42	27	30
36	Manchester Business School	UK	46	21	38	26
37	Univ. of North Carolina – Kenan-Flagler	USA	19	25	51	42
38	EM Lyon	France	43	28	19	43

Rank	Business School Name	Country	Website Rank	Facebook Rank	Twitter Rank	LinkedIn Rank
39	Univ. of Toronto – Rotman	Canada	13	46	35	33
40	Carnegie Mellon – Tepper	USA	15	36	36	44
41	HEC Paris	France	39	43	41	20
42	Emory Univ. – Goizueta	USA	27	30	32	49
43	Univ. of Cape Town GSB	South Africa	31	44	18	52
44	Dartmouth College – Tuck	USA	28	41	33	47
45	Univ. of W. Ontario – Ivey	Canada	51	48	29	34
46	NUS School of Business	Singapore	23	44	48	37
47	Georgetown Univ. – McDonough	USA	50	22	50	50
48	ESMT Germany	Germany	52	27	40	51
49	St Gallen	Switzerland	40	50	31	45
50	CEIBS	China	41	51	42	38

SHOULD I EVEN CONSIDER LOWER-RANKED SCHOOLS?

B-school rankings have their own parameters to judge schools. A candidate's yardstick may be very different. So, whether a school is rung 2 or 3 is a very subjective viewpoint. There are many excellent schools that might not figure in the top rankings. But they are well respected in their region. They have several thousand (if not tens of thousands of) graduates who have gone on to work for reputed corporate brands or started their own ventures.

For my basic graduation degree, I went to a local ('un-hyped') engineering college that doesn't feature in any domestic or global rankings. But it gave me a good education and I did pretty well for myself career-wise.

Extending that logic, I'd say, 'Don't shortlist or discard B-schools purely on the basis of rankings.'

Many aspirants ask: *'Should I apply to Harvard? Isn't it the best school in the world?'*

While selecting B-schools, variations of this question pop up in the minds of MBA applicants. Other queries falling in a similar category are:

- Which is the best two-year (or one-year) MBA programme?
- Are US universities better than those in the UK or Europe?
- Should I choose international business schools over Indian MBA colleges?

All these questions are natural and justified, considering how much you would be investing in the programme. Ask Indian applicants and most would say IIM Ahmedabad (IIM-A) is the best Indian MBA programme in the two-year format. Or that ISB is the best GMAT-based Indian MBA programme. Or that Harvard is the best two-year MBA course in the world.

But if you really look beyond the popular opinion, for many of these questions, there are no absolute answers really. There's one basic quality that applies to B-schools – uniqueness. All MBA programmes are not created equal. So there is no 'best' that applies to everyone.

Contrast this with the GMAT, where the objective for all test takers is exactly the same: score a balanced and high GMAT score. The GMAT syllabus is fixed. The duration of the test is fixed. How you study for the GMAT might vary – self-study using GMAT books, online GMAT course, classroom- based GMAT coaching or one-on-one tutoring for specific GMAT topics (for example, verbal). But that doesn't change the fact that there's exactly one goal for everyone. Crack the test and come out victorious.

For Adcoms too, it's a like-to-like comparison to find out which GMAT score is better. A 780 score is better than a 700 score. No debate there.

However, consider the bigger picture now for the MBA degree. Almost everything about it is variable. Apart from the three-letter acronym that you'll get on your résumé, everything that goes into getting it varies. The duration of the MBA programme, the syllabus, the teaching methodology (mix of classroom-based lectures, group assignments, presentations, case studies).

Most importantly, the takeaways from the MBA experience are different for every single person.

Not everyone wants to be an investment banker (or a management consultant).

Not everyone wants to work in the US (or India or Europe).

Not everyone wants to spend two years in a classroom (or maybe even a single day).

Not everyone is there for the academic knowledge (which you could get from books anyway).

Not everyone wants to earn a lot of money and buy a home in the Bahamas.

Well, on second thoughts, ignore that last point for now.

In such a situation, where almost all parameters that you could compare vary so dramatically, can you really compare two schools and say one is better than the other? MBA rankings try to do exactly that, and I think many of them raise more eyebrows than provide solutions (global truths) that would make everyone happy.

I use Harvard only as an example to illustrate the point. I greatly respect the brand, but I just can't afford it. Whether they'd take me is a different story, but apart from MBA financing issues, there was no way I could've met my post-MBA goal (voluntary retirement from corporate life before I turned forty) if I had gone to Harvard.

So let's ignore the general public vote and rephrase the original question. Which is the best business school in the world...for *you*?

And to arrive at the answer, you'll have to ask yourself a whole lot of questions about where you are in your career right now, why you are unhappy, where you want to go from here, and which MBA can get you there in the most painless possible manner.

You can identify many of the gaps and issues and come up with the answers on your own. The key is to start early, have access to the right data/information, and design a customized application strategy plan (covering B-schools, positioning your profile, planning out the post-MBA career, etc.) that works for you.

I work with several candidates each year who want to know: 'If I don't get into the Top-10 ranked B-schools, should I even bother?' And in many cases, the answer is 'Yes, you should.' You should look at a mix of schools which may not be top-ranked, but which offer excellent resources to help you break into the industry and role that you desire.

For instance, if you are interested in Supply Chain Management (SCM), you'll find many of the top schools offering a specialization in this field – MIT Sloan, Wharton, Kellogg. But lower-ranked schools like Fisher (Ohio State University), Smeal (Penn State University) and Broad (Michigan State University) are good at SCM too.

Of course, the brands aren't comparable. But the silver lining is that the cost of attending these programmes is significantly lower. Many of the folks we've helped to get into these schools have got a generous amount of MBA scholarships. In the five-to-ten-year horizon, the RoI calculations can look very different for students of these schools.

Appendix H
How to Prepare for the GMAT

WHAT GMAT PREP MATERIAL SHOULD YOU USE

As the GMAT format has changed, many of the old GMAT preparation guides may not be as helpful to crack the GMAT syllabus as the latest ones, if you are tackling the new GMAT format.

Some prefer joining a class as it adds structure and discipline to the preparation phase. Others prefer a do-it-yourself approach by buying some good GMAT books and creating a flexible and personalized self-study plan. Take a call based on your personal preference.

The Official Guide for GMAT Review

If you are going for only one book, this one wins the fight. *The Official Guide for GMAT Review* (go for the latest edition) might be the single most important resource that you can have in your GMAT preparation process. Many call it the GMAT prep Bible, and not without reason. Among all the GMAT books available in the market, the *Official Guide* (13th Edition) is the only book to include real GMAT questions for practice.

Most other GMAT coaching books create their own GMAT practice questions that mimic or are 'inspired' by the official GMAT guide.

Manhattan GMAT Strategy Guides (Eight Books)

This one's for beginners who have the capacity and the patience to go through eight separate GMAT prep books. They'll help you build a good foundation of concepts used in each section of the GMAT syllabus.

The individual guides are also available separately if you need help only with specific weak areas.

Kaplan GMAT 800: Advanced Prep for Advanced Students

If you thought the other guides were too easy, Kaplan raises the bar with this guide. You might want to pick this up after you've completed the GMAT *Official Guide*.

The Official Guide for GMAT Quantitative Review

Though this book does have several sample GMAT questions that go beyond the primary GMAT *Official Guide*, you may not want to go for both. Instead, you could get the basics sorted out with the *OG13* and then look for an advanced-level guide for the quantitative section.

Kaplan GMAT Math Workbook

There have been lukewarm responses to this guide. Some have found it to be good to get the basics in place. Others who were expecting many more difficult 700–750+ questions have not been too impressed.

The Official Guide for GMAT Verbal Review

This verbal guide continues the good work done by the GMAT *Official Guide*. There are more real GMAT questions to give you practice on how the real test would feel like. Don't jump into these before getting the verbal concepts clarified.

Manhattan GMAT Sentence Correction Strategy Guide

GMAT Sentence Correction is a painful area for most non-native test takers. The Manhattan SC guide has been a favourite among Indian and international MBA applicants for several years.

Kaplan GMAT Verbal Workbook

This book, just like Kaplan's quantitative guide, tries to go beyond the basics. It's a good option for folks who want to get an understanding of various verbal sections and how to use advanced strategies to tackle verbal questions.

Download the Free GMAT Preparation Software

You can download the free GMAT software – GMATPrep from MBA.com – to prepare and train for the test.

The GMATPrep software includes two full-length CATs (computer adaptive tests) that are a very good approximation of your GMAT score if you were to take it with your current level of practice and competence. It also comes with answers to each question, but unfortunately, it does not include explanations of the underlying concepts.

What About the Free GMAT Prep Material on the Internet?

There's a whole lot of 'free' material available on the Internet that GMAT test takers seem to love. But there are several things you should be aware of, if that thought has crossed your mind.

'*I've got 50 MB of the best GMAT preparation material with me, good GMAT verbal and quantitative questions, full-length exam software… downloaded for free from the Internet. Plus my friends gave me another 25 MB of practice questions. I think that is more than enough for anyone to crack the GMAT. Right, sir?*' The twenty-four-year-old candidate from Chennai asked me excitedly on the phone, as if he had stumbled upon a gold mine. And he was definitely not the first one to come up with that question.

Apart from copyright and IPR infringement issues which he was completely ignorant (?) about, he was also missing another bigger point. Several interrelated ones actually.

Accuracy and Credibility Issues

Free content does not necessarily translate into accurate content. People download GMAT verbal questions, quantitative questions, complete courses, free full-length GMAT tests and all other variations that you can imagine. Many are shocked to see mistakes in the answers and, at times, in the questions too.

QUANTITY VS QUALITY

Brute force will not help you score high on the GMAT. A few hundred well-chosen GMAT questions can improve your score more than a random collection of thousands. Check out the blogs of folks who have got high GMAT scores. Their 'How I scored a 750+ post' will invariably include a diligently created study plan that they customized according to their personal needs.

Inconsistent Levels of Difficulty

The set of questions created by one GMAT test prep team (free or otherwise) can be dramatically different from another team's content. No wonder then the students get a 740 in one test, 630 in another and then 760 in the third one. Training the brain to tackle GMAT questions is more a matter of getting the fundamentals sorted out and then digging into practice questions with gradually increasing levels of difficulty. That's how sports training also works – if you want to build muscle mass you don't jump from 5 pound dumbbells to 25 pounds ones and then back to 15 pounds.

Despite the huge amount of free exam resources that they've collected by legit or dubious means, many candidates fail to reach their target scores. The reasons for their bad performance have a lot to do with the points listed above.

Of course, you don't need to sign up for any class or online course if you can manage it on your own. But do follow one 'system' with dedication, structure and discipline.

HOW TO OVERCOME GMAT TEST ANXIETY

A lot of us experience anxiety whenever we take up a new task or are subject to an unfamiliar environment. In the GMAT, considering that the stakes are high, it is common to suffer from test anxiety which is likely to adversely affect your output. Anxiety management may not completely take care of the pre-test jitters but can surely go a long way towards reducing your stress and improving your performance.

Here are a few tips that may prove handy:

1. Be Confident

It is good to aim high but remember that the GMAT is not the only qualifying criteria to get into a good B-school. You can work harder on the other elements and present an impressive application. So, do not burden yourself by aiming for unrealistic or extremely high scores. Remember that the GMAT can be taken multiple times and the highest score is considered for the MBA application. So even if you do not perform well in the first attempt, there's always a second chance. While retaking the GMAT, you would have already gone through the whole process once and would be in a better position to handle your anxieties. With a better GMAT preparation strategy, you have a good chance to score higher. Do not get pressured with thoughts about what others will think if you get a low GMAT score. You can perform better when you leave behind all the baggage (literally and figuratively) at the door and enter your exam hall with a fresh mind and an empty bladder. Be positive, have faith in yourself and think that you will do your best.

2. Exercise

Exercise not just keeps you physically fit but reduces stress as well. So it's good if you can take some time off for this in your daily schedule. Work out a sweat, but that doesn't mean you kill yourself by enrolling in that upcoming marathon. Exercise till you reach the *feel-good* state as opposed to *I'm-gonna-collapse-somebody-pick-me-up-and-take-me-home* state.

3. Get Familiar with What to Anticipate on the Test Day

Read the information provided on the official GMAT website (mba.com) thoroughly.

It provides all the information you need about how things are at the exam, and the various rules and regulations. This has also been documented in the form of a video on YouTube. The video is titled 'GMAT Test Center – A Guide to Success when taking the GMAT.' Make sure you see it a few times. Familiarity with the process itself can help relieve a lot of test-related anxiety.

4. Keep Your Handy Stuff Ready

Keep your bag ready beforehand. Make a final checklist of what to take along and what to avoid. Keep your documents and IDs ready. Also carry along a light snack (maybe a cereal bar or some fruit) that you would like to have during your short breaks. Keep a list of at least five schools ready where you would wish to forward your GMAT scores without any fee. Thereafter you would be charged for any additional school you wish to forward your scores to.

5. Be in Good Shape for the Test

Prepare a planner for your GMAT study routine. If you are working, try squeezing out at least one or two hours in the morning before you go to work and a few hours in the evening if possible. If that's difficult and you're entirely dependent on your weekends, make it a point to keep a dedicated time on the weekends for studying. Time management should be done efficiently so that you are able to cover the entire GMAT syllabus and solve sufficient practice questions. Devote additional time for your weak areas where you can improve with practice.

Follow a structured approach and stick to a regular study regime; leave time towards the end for practice tests. This would help you get used to the test format and the lengthy duration. Take the sample tests provided free of cost by mba.com towards the end which would simulate the actual GMAT exam. This would also give an idea of how well prepared you are and what score to expect.

6. Relax and Rest

Now you know that you are all set, so just take your mind off the test and relax. Preferably, be done with it all and keep the last two to three days before the exam as stress-free as possible. If you feel you're too restless, try doing meditation. Practice deep breathing and relaxation techniques, which would also help you maintain your cool during the GMAT test.

KNOW WHEN TO STOP LOOKING FOR NEW TIPS AND MOVE ON

Speaking of tips, while some of the GMAT preparation sites have good practical advice, a whole lot of them come up with gems that make you go…hmmm, not so elementary, Dr Watson!

Here's a sampling of some often-beaten-to-death GMAT preparation tips that might seem familiar, maybe because you've read some of them elsewhere (in this book?).

- *Practice a lot before you take the real test*

This is just to discourage those who were planning to explore the wonderful world of Computer Adaptive Testing on the day of the test.

- *Pace yourself well through the test*

And just to clarify, we aren't talking about treadmills or spot jogging.

- *Don't waste your time during the test*

Which roughly translates to: no ogling at the babe on the next computer, no Sudoku practice and definitely no push-ups to firm up your pectoral muscles. All that can wait till you've completed the test.

- *Get enough rest before the exam*

What this means is you need to avoid highly strenuous activities the night before and avoid performance-enhancing products, including those that start with V and end up at Agra.

- *Avoid distractions and focus on your PC*

Interpretation: Avoid looking at the answers being selected by the guy-on-the-adjacent-PC. His answers (or for that matter, questions) will not be the same as yours.

- *Be alert during the test*

Don't leave your footwear at the door. You'll spend less time worrying (about whether the guy who completed the test before you will walk away with your new Reeboks) and more time focussing on the test.

- *Wear comfortable clothes for the test*

Meaning: No Batman, Superman or any other superhero costumes that involve wearing outerwear before innerwear.

Most books and websites resort to a little bit of fluff and padding here and there to beef up the content. But when the fluff exceeds the real useful content, it's time to move on to another site.

Appendix I
How to Write Impactful MBA Essays

How to Avoid the Common Pitfalls While Writing MBA Essays

It's a relief to be done with the GMAT preparation and move on to the main MBA application. The most ominous part now is to write the MBA essays. The best-written MBA essays can open up the doors to the final round – MBA interviews. But, for many, an interview may never happen as the admission committee has already made up its mind (based on your essays) that you aren't good enough for their programme for that year.

You may have done your research on what you should do when it comes to MBA essays. However, it's also a good idea to have the knowledge of what to avoid in your MBA essays so that you don't inadvertently shoot yourself in the foot. So here's a list of eight things to keep in mind while working on your MBA application.

1. Avoid Repetition (Or, in Other Words, er, Avoid Repetition)

You don't need to discuss how you managed to pull through with a high GMAT score or other obvious facts already presented on your résumé or the main application form. Use the essays to your advantage by presenting fresh content. Build upon the objective data that you've presented and don't just repackage the same content. If you feel you've reached saturation point, take a break, and start afresh later when the ideas flow more freely.

2. Do Not Use Fancy Words or Sentence Constructs

Admission committees have to handle loads of applications, and they aren't hunting for the next Shakespeare in their review process. So don't try to impress them by forcibly fitting in fancy words or smart-sounding idioms into your essays. Don't use your creativity in creating complex and awkward statements that would make it difficult for the admission committee to figure out what you're trying to say.

3. Do Not Go Off-track

MBA essay questions and topics are very focussed. Which, unfortunately, means that you may not have a chance to talk about many things that you might have wanted to share with the admissions committee. Don't think of the MBA word count as a blank canvas where you can fit in irrelevant pieces of information. If it isn't related to the question asked, keep it out. The reviewer would value relevant answers rather than impressive but unrelated excerpts from your past.

You may be able to provide all that additional interesting data in your optional essay. But again, don't use that essay as a general dumping ground.

4. Don't Abuse Word Limits

Don't think of word counts as something that you can manage at the last minute after you are done pouring out your life history. Bear in mind the word count and be precise in answering the question asked so that you don't have to edit out a big chunk from your writing effort. We have more on this topic a little later.

5. Avoid Reiteration from the B-school Website

Adcoms know what is there on the website. They also know that you have read the website. In an attempt to prove that you're a great fit for a particular school, don't try to over-focus on a particular quality the school holds high regard for. Some candidates assume using the words and phrases used on the website will be an easy way to demonstrate 'FIT'. There is no automated programme reviewing your application to count the phrase density match. But there is one for plagiarism checking. So don't copy-paste content from the official B-school website or from samples that you've found from other sources. Narrate *your* story.

6. Don't Do a Rush Job

Before you get called for the MBA interview, your essays are doing the talking for you. They tell the B-school reviewer about your past achievements, future goals, reasons for doing an MBA. They create the initial impression about you. So take the time to think about what goes into those essays. Which means a whole lot of time strategizing, structuring and planning for the essays. The writing part will become easier. Don't be in a hurry to get done with your essays.

7. Avoid Superlatives

Avoid mentioning that you are a super-achiever or a person with exceptional skills or talent. Even if it is true, it'll sound as if you are bragging. Instead, narrate incidents that would actually reflect this quality of yours and give the admissions committee a chance to make up their mind about how good you are and what qualities set you apart. Give them content and facts. Allow them to use their judgement in deciding whether you are good or fantastic.

8. Don't End Up with a 'Loser' Tag

Transparency is good but not when it ends up showing you as a loser. Avoid mentioning repeatedly about the various failures you have encountered in life. Failures must be viewed positively, as a chance to know where to be cautious, learn what could have been better and move one step higher. You are a better person because of the roadblocks you've hit in life.

9. Avoid Over-emphasizing Your Ambitious Future Plans

Unless you've been asked about your career goals, try not to keep talking about your great plans for the distant future in every essay. Your credibility lies in how much you've achieved and that's what the admission committee is more interested in rather than reading about your ambitions or aspirations which are difficult to evaluate.

The devil lies in the detail and these are just a few aspects to keep in mind when you start working on your MBA essays.

Appendix J
How to Create an Impressive Résumé

What's the best way to form a great first impression on an influential decision maker? Create an impactful curriculum vitae (CV). This applies to almost all situations where a résumé will be used as one of the tools to filter a huge list of candidates. Whether you are creating an MBA résumé format for B-school applications or creating a CV for internships or jobs, there are a few basic things you can keep in mind to maximize the impact.

There are differences between the MBA résumé and a regular job résumé.

Let's cover the basic principles that'll help you in your MBA résumé as well as your job résumé.

We'll cover this in three stages: First we look at the process that a majority of applicants generally follow, then we change perspectives and look at the process that a reviewer is likely to follow. Once we have compared the two, the disconnect is easier to locate. Based on that you'd know what you should or should not do when you create your résumé.

WHAT IS THE TYPICAL WAY CANDIDATES WRITE A RÉSUMÉ?

- Most candidates start the process by searching for sample résumés and freely downloadable CV creation templates and samples. The focus is on getting the best-looking CV. The font style and size, the margins, the spacing, the sections all become important.
- The second instinctive urge is to try and cram as much data as

possible into the (implicitly or explicitly) imposed size limits. If there are no size limits, the freedom often gets abused.

I've seen résumés that run into ten-plus pages, complete with pictures, designed borders and colours that'll make the wild 1960s look tame in comparison. Fortunately, I haven't seen any scented ones that were sealed with a kiss. Either they are no longer in vogue or folks are keeping them for other occasions.

How Would the Résumé Reader Review and Evaluate Your CV?

- In case you are applying for competitive positions (like applications to MBA programmes, high-paying jobs), especially those with deadlines, your résumé will probably go through multiple rounds of review. Very few applicants will have the pleasure and honour of discussing their CV with the reviewer over coffee while watching the sun set over the horizon.

- In the crazy rush to skim through the pile of résumés lying on the desk, the first level of review will probably be done not by the final decision maker, but by someone who's more junior. The role of this first-level reviewer will be quite simple. Spend as little time as possible to speed-read each CV and either dump it or move it to the next level for further review.

- The ones that move to the next level would generally have some key attributes that need to stand out. The more of those parameters you have, the better your chances of getting promoted to the subsequent level(s) of review. In fact, it is common practice for the first-level reviewers to just highlight or encircle the words and numbers that really matter on your résumé (we'll soon come to what these are).

- After the initial screening, when the pile of submitted CVs reaches a more manageable level, the decision makers will start getting involved. Each résumé will get a little more time, for a complete and independent review by a senior member of the selection team.

- If the final reviewer (an admissions committee member or your future boss) is convinced that the traits he or she is looking for are present to a large extent, then the coffee and sunset scenario becomes more likely. If you've compared the two, the disconnect should become more apparent. If not, let's get more specific about what you should be doing.

How Should you Go about Writing a Résumé?

Highlight the important parameters:

- Brand names: Strong brands convey more than words. If you've studied in a top university or worked in top brand companies, ensure that those names stand out (make them bold).
- If grades (your undergraduate GPA[1] or your postgraduate percentage) and competitive test scores (like GMAT, TOEFL) are relevant, add them. Many management consulting firms look at these numbers to filter out candidates.
- Evaluate the mix of technical (using strategy frameworks, financial modelling, requirements analysis and design, risk management) and non-technical skills (for example, leadership potential, managerial ability, people skills) that the reviewer is expecting in the résumé. Ensure that your résumé clearly mentions how and where you displayed those traits. The lesser the learning curve for you in the new role, the faster and more productive you will be. Convince your recruiter (or admissions committee) that you'd be able to pull your own weight.
- Use short sentences (bullet points work well) in describing your contribution in each role. Verbose text only acts as a filler and takes up important space on your CV, without conveying the important qualities. In fact, if you aren't careful while writing the résumé content, the strong points might get lost in the details.
- What you've done in the past is important. But how that has prepared you for the next role is more critical. So present your accomplishments in a way that makes the reviewer's job easier. One way to do that is by using action verbs (managed, coordinated, led,

---

[1] GPA (short for Grade Point Average) is a measure of academic performance. Unlike the percentage system that Indian students are familiar with, the GPA is more popular in the US.

planned, analysed). More than just being verbs, they communicate the skill that you demonstrated.

- Rather than do just a dry listing of what anybody in that previous role would've done, make it look more like your personal story.
- And try to do all of this in one page. If you think that's not practical, maybe you can add another page. But that's it. Don't convert your résumé into a novel. The length of your CV is inversely proportional to the attention span of the reviewer.

The bottom line is that the content in your résumé is far more important than the CV format you use. Writing a short, crisp and impactful résumé can be tougher than you think. So get a good format going and keep fine-tuning it over time. You'll soon find a personalized CV format that works best for you compared to the thousands of sample résumé formats available for free download on the Internet.

Appendix K
How to Manage Recommendations

A commonly known fact (assuming you've read the application guidelines on B-school websites) is that your MBA application will be looked at as a complete package and the impact that it'll have on the admissions committee will depend on each of the components included. But candidates often discard that guideline and create their own priority list. There's a clear pecking order while they work on their MBA applications – a preferential treatment for GMAT preparation, with the MBA essays coming in at a distant second and the letters of recommendations (LORs) often being sidelined.

You may have an enviable GMAT score, but that tells the admission committee nothing about your work-related accomplishments and business potential. And you think some decent essays will do the job, if you can structure and present your work-related experiences in an impressive manner. But it's all from a single perspective – yours.

Recommendations are the only window for the admissions committee to get a feel for what 'others' think about you. So a little foresight and planning can help you get this aspect in good shape too.

WHY GIVE IMPORTANCE TO THE LORs?

1. This is the only component that provides the admissions committee an external perspective about your area of expertise, skills, capabilities or areas where you excel (when compared to your co-workers).

2. All the good things about you would sound like a boast if mentioned by you. When the same comes from an authentic outside source, it gets more credibility.

3. Though some parts of the LOR may have an overlap with the MBA essays and résumé, it would actually verify the claims you've made or the facts you've mentioned. It gives the admissions committee more reason to view your application positively.

So What Can You Do About Your Letter of Recommendation?

- Plan in advance:

Most of the B-schools ask for two recommendations (however, at Harvard, three are required). The format varies for each school and so do the questions. Completing the recommendations can be time-consuming, so it would be advisable to start thinking about who your recommendations would be from and approach them well in advance. This way your recommenders won't be pressured about a specific time-frame within which they have to complete your recommendation. Give them some breathing space.

- Keep aside time for discussions:

You cannot just hand over the job to your recommender and sit with your fingers crossed and expect a fantastic output. There has to be some proactive effort on your part too. You should be able to spend time in discussions, briefing them about your line of thoughts: why you're planning for an MBA, what your post-MBA goals are and how an MBA from a particular B-school would help. You can let them browse through your essays and a well-written résumé. The LORs would then be in sync with your entire application and the recommender would be in a position to point out how you would be a good fit for the schools you've chosen.

- Provide important bullet points:

Don't assume that that your recommenders have a sharp memory and remember exactly all the details of the projects you've worked on with them. Chances are, they don't. You can help them out by providing bullet points of the various projects you've worked on, and where you may have shown some exceptional ability by meeting tough deadlines, successfully leading a team, bringing in substantial revenue to the company or bagging a contract for your company by using your marketing skills. A variety of instances demonstrating your dynamic personality would help spice up your application.

The LOR should be able to point out instances during your career span which highlight at least a few of the following aspects:

1. Technical expertise
2. Analytical skills
3. Time management skills
4. People management or team-leading ability
5. Ability to acclimatize to new environment
6. Adaptability to new skills
7. Spirit to motivate your team
8. Marketing skills
9. Ethics
10. Communication skills within or outside the team as required

• Keep an eye on the application timeline:
It is essential to keep your recommenders updated about the progress and status of your MBA application so that they are reminded of the various deadlines and are able to keep your LORs ready.

Keep these points in mind as you start working on your next set of applications. As with essays, you will realize the mistakes you've made with the earlier recommenders and recommendation process. So learn, rectify and re-attack.

Appendix L
How to Prepare for MBA Interviews

MBA interviews generally tend to focus on the story that the candidate has submitted. This could be about the applicant's achievements, the rationale/timing for an MBA, post-MBA goals and other aspects covered in the résumé or essays. So it's very important that you know your application inside out. Also prepare for questions that may be indirectly related to the facts, claims and accomplishments you have listed in the application.

Apart from the grilling related to the application content, you can expect situational interview questions. These are the vague, mysterious and confusing interview questions that get thrown at you when you are trying to get into the best B-schools. Or, for that matter, management consulting (including the top-tier strategy consulting firms) and investment banking jobs as well.

They make you feel that the tough technical questions you got for your first few jobs were so much easier in comparison. At least there was a right or wrong answer to them, and after the interview you'd know if you fared well or not. With situational interviews, most candidates are unsure of how their performance will be judged.

What are Situational Interview Questions?

These are questions designed to probe into your behavioural/thought process. These questions allow the interviewer to find out how you have dealt with (or would deal with) certain situations at work or outside. It gives the recruiter an insight into your personality and your working style. The questions could be in the area of interpersonal skills, analytical ability, capacity to work under stress, problem solving, multitasking skills or other aspects.

WHY DO COMPANIES ASK SITUATIONAL INTERVIEW QUESTIONS?

Your résumé contains a listing of all the important milestones and achievements that you'd like your future employer to know. But that little document does not allow the recruiter to judge what challenges you faced while working towards those milestones. They can also extrapolate these inputs to get a feel for how you would perform when faced with new challenges that your previous job hasn't allowed you to tackle.

HOW TO ANSWER SITUATIONAL INTERVIEW QUESTIONS?

For each question that you encounter, before impatiently jumping into an answer, ask yourself these additional questions:

- What is the interviewer really trying to get out of this question?
- What kind of skills would I need to talk about to convince the recruiter that I have what it takes to be successful in the new role (just like I was in the previous ones)?
- How can I answer this question with concrete evidence, rather than offering vague and diplomatic responses?

SAMPLE SITUATIONAL INTERVIEW QUESTIONS

Here are some examples of situational interview questions. Think about how you would structure your answer to each of these using the three sub-question approach.

- Can you think of a situation where you had a conflict with a difficult colleague? How did you deal with the situation?
- Did you ever face a situation where you had to motivate yourself to accomplish something?
- Were you criticized at work? Why? How did you react?
- Describe a situation where you failed to deliver. How did you deal with it?

- Have you faced a situation where the majority was in favour of a certain decision and you were not convinced about it? What did you do in that situation?
- Give us an example of a situation where you had to take a decision based on very little (or too much) data.
- How did you manage to achieve work-life balance in your previous jobs?
- Have there been situations where you had to come up with an unconventional approach to solve a problem?
- Was there a time when you were faced with too many tasks with stringent deadlines, where each was as important as the other?
- Can you think of examples where you used non-technical skills to make an impact on your organization?

Appendix M
About MBA Crystal Ball

In the first edition of this book, apart from a single reference on the author introduction page, there was absolutely nothing that covered my primary role as an admissions consultant or my consulting venture, MBA Crystal Ball. I felt then that it would be good to keep the book neutral and not appear as if I've written it to promote my business. There was also the teeny-weeny concern that the book might actually turn off people from approaching me offline.

But interestingly, I realized that the book was having some unintended (but positive) consequences. It had become a tool to filter out applicants who were really serious about getting into the top B-schools.

Reading all the not-so-easy-to-digest content in the earlier chapters actually made many Indian applicants re-evaluate their expectations and approach. These are the folks who became our best clients as we didn't have to spend too much time convincing them about having practical expectations from their MBA experience.

So, in this edition, I thought it was pointless to segregate the author avatar from the admission consultant. There's no identity crisis here. It's the same guy delivering the same message:

'If you are practical about your expectations from an MBA, I'll help you with the execution.'

The first half of the message is addressed by the book. The second half is addressed by MBA Crystal Ball (MCB). So I've included a short introduction about my venture in this edition.

Before talking about MCB and its basic philosophy, it's important to provide some context.

Here's an unsettling fact: Indian MBA applicants are more likely to be rejected by the top B-schools.

Most MBA applicants think their chances of getting into a top MBA programme is purely dependent on the strength of the application and has nothing to do with their nationality. Not true, says John Byrne, former executive editor of *BusinessWeek* and founder of Poets & Quants (P&Q), a leading and highly respectable MBA portal. According to him the rejection rates for Indian candidates are '*dramatically higher*' than for any other nationality[1].

An Indian applicant is three to five times less likely to get an offer compared to domestic candidates from the US. In fact, European and Latin American candidates would also fare better than Indians. What makes the P&Q survey results extremely credible is the fact that the data has been supplied officially by B-schools to Bloomberg *BusinessWeek*.

Some schools that feature in the survey include prestigious names like MIT (Sloan), Fuqua (Duke University), Ross (Michigan), Purdue (Krannert), Olin (Washington University), Vanderbilt (Owen), University of Southern California's Marshall and others.

Let's take an example of one of the top ten business schools to understand the basic concept.

Assumptions:

- Class size = 250
- Number of applications received = 1,000
  - Domestic applications = 300
  - International applications = 700
    - Indian applications = 220
    - China + other Asian countries = 200
- Overall selectivity = 25 per cent

The selectivity number indicates that one in every four applicants will get in. However, if you assume that this selectivity number is applicable to all nationalities, that's not true.

---

[1] Poets & Quants Survey: http://poetsandquants.com/2011/11/19/indian-chinese-mba-applicants-face-higher-rejection/

Continuing with our example above, the selectivity figures for various nationalities would be as follows:

- Chinese applicants: 10 per cent
- European applicants: 39 per cent
- American applicants: 39 per cent
- Latin American applicants: 26 per cent
- Middle East applicants: 26 per cent
- And the selectivity for Indians is a whopping [*drumroll begins*]...8 *per cent*!

This is significantly lower than the class average of 25 per cent.

Of course, these are numbers from the survey to convey the idea of what P&Q might have been trying to say. Factors like yield (accepted to offered ratio) aren't being discussed in the survey. The actual percentages may vary for each school.

The million (or considering MBA tuition costs, maybe it's a 100,000–150,000) dollar question – why is it happening to Indian candidates?

B-schools and recruiters cited several reasons ranging from the need to maintain class diversity to language issues. But the main point relevant for Indian candidates was the dependency on gaining work permit visas after graduation. Admission officers are trying to put themselves in the shoes of recruiters and filtering out potentially high-maintenance candidates who'd have a tough time getting MBA jobs after graduation. The best option is to nip the problem in the bud.

For you as an Indian candidate, remember that the competition (much like charity) begins at home. You will first compete with your beloved (and not to mention extremely competitive) countrymen. Then, if you survive, the competition gets bigger and tougher as other nationalities come into the fray. That's how the game works.

Apart from your GMAT preparation and B-school selection efforts, start thinking about your career plans as well. See how an international B-school will be able to get you closer to your target industry and role. Think about it from the admission officer's perspective and try to address their questions and concerns.

THE MOCK APPLICATION PROCESS

When I was working on my own MBA application, I had no access to such statistics. But I did read many discussions on various MBA forums where Indian applicants with strong profiles shared the disappointing news about their rejections. I thought it was unfair that Indians, despite the potential, were not able to approach the extremely competitive international MBA admissions in the right manner, while others who were earning in dollars, pounds and euros could engage international MBA admissions consulting firms and strengthen their application further.

My GMAT score was quite low (by Indian standards) and I knew that I had to make the rest of my application as strong as possible. So I focused on my essays, résumé, recommendations and interview. Ultimately, all the research and effort paid off. I got into my top choice B-school with scholarships. That's when I realized that when B-schools say they look at each profile holistically, they are serious about it.

That prompted me to launch MBA Crystal Ball (MCB) to make it a level playing field – at least for the small number of applicants I could help out. Most of the candidates who come to MCB have excellent credentials – many of them are from the IITs and most have some fantastic corporate experience to talk about. But they also have big question marks on the approach as they just don't know how and what to present in their applications. Our undergraduate education doesn't train us to address the introspective (at times, almost philosophical) topics that business schools ask for.

I saw that applicants were spending two to three months on GMAT preparation, but underestimating the importance of the other aspects – essays, recommendations, résumé, interview, academic performance. Considering all those components, the GMAT score might roughly have a 20 per cent weight in the process. Effectively, applicants were spending 80 per cent of their preparatory effort on 20 per cent of the MBA application. They were ignoring the rest and assuming that they'd be able to submit their best application to the top schools with little or no practice. All the forums and MBA books were giving them knowledge about what they should be doing in essays and interviews. But there was no real way for them to polish and test out their execution skills.

The multiple mock tests that simulated the real GMAT test helped students in identifying weak areas. Students could then focus specifically on those areas and strengthen them. But there was no such simulation for the rest of the application.

I thought it might help to have a similar simulation process for the non-GMAT part of the MBA application too, where candidates could practise their application skills in a risk-free environment.

So, in the first year of MBA Crystal Ball, I conceptualized what I call the MBA Mock Application Process (MBA MAP, in short). The basic idea was similar to the GMAT mock tests. I make students go through a mini-application. In the first half of the process, I play the role of an admissions officer and evaluate their mini-applications from multiple angles. In the second half, I become the counsellor and work with the candidate to highlight the gaps, inconsistencies and impracticalities in the applicant's strategy.

After this highly introspective exercise, candidates become more familiar with their strengths and weaknesses. They have more credible answers to questions – 'Is the MBA right for me?', 'What am I expecting from an MBA?', 'Are my goals practical?', 'What makes me better compared to the thousands of other applicants who are vying for an admission seat at the top B-school?'

This puts them in a much better situation while submitting the actual applications, compared to others who are following the traditional approach of jumping into top B-school applications with no practice. In a few cases, at the end of the MBA MAP exercise, I've asked candidates to defer or cancel their MBA plans too.

Through word-of-mouth publicity, the MBA MAP became very popular. In fact, it has become the flagship product of MBA Crystal Ball. Folks who were apprehensive about the value of admissions consulting (thanks to the mass market approach that has dominated the Indian market) started seeing the value in premium consulting. We started offering the regular services like essay reviews, interview preparation and general career counselling for those facing a mid-career crisis.

Each year, MBA Crystal Ball consultants help a select few applicants significantly change the odds in their favour compared to the industry average. Several have got generous MBA scholarships too. That convinced me that we were on to something interesting here, which had more potential than I initially imagined.

Over time, the website (www.mbacrystalball.com) has grown in popularity. The blog and the discussion forum now host a large amount of free MBA and career resources that have been created specially for the Indian MBA applicant. It attracts a huge volume of traffic from across the world.

Much of it doesn't make money for me. Many might question the commercial rationale for sharing all that knowledge for free. Apart from just being a vehicle for us to sell our consulting services, the MBA Crystal Ball platform has taken on a bigger role in collating and disseminating knowledge that was difficult to obtain on international forums that were primarily meant for the Western audience. Do check it out when you have the time, and share your feedback with me on what you like or don't like. And, more importantly, what would make it better.

MBA Crystal Ball has a very small team of MBA consultants. Unlike bigger teams with a corporate set-up, our capacity is limited. We run a for-profit venture (otherwise a whole lot of the non-revenue-earning work we do will not be sustainable) but with a social enterprise flavour. Money is important for us, but we haven't allowed it to be the primary driver for growth.

I left a lucrative corporate job a few years back to focus full-time on MBA Crystal Ball. I work much harder than I've ever worked in a 'regular' job. But just between you and me, in terms of money, I still make only a fraction of what I was making in my mergers and acquisitions role. Maybe over time that situation will change. Maybe it won't. But I have no complaints at all as it's been a fantastic experience so far.

The journey has been exciting, challenging and at times scary as well. One week before I wrote this appendix, I spent almost an hour on an impromptu call, talking to someone (I still have no clue about his real identity) who had reached out anonymously over email to say he was feeling suicidal due to the perception (enforced by his family and society) that he was a professional failure. As I suggested ways to get his career back on track, I tried to act as if I was in complete control, but my heart was possibly pounding faster than his. I heard back from him a few days later saying he was following up on some of the suggestions from the call. I hope his story ends well.

Though this was an extreme case, from the comments and queries we get on our blog and forum, it seems that there's a lot of pain, depression and anxiety even among the educated, capable professionals in the country. Though our focus has primarily been on MBA admissions, the MCB website has become more of an interactive platform for reaching out and giving back to a wider community.

The Indian applicant community needs more mentors. If you get into a top university, I'd like you to share your experiences with the others through our blog and forum. I am always looking out for interesting and inspiring stories for our site. You can connect with me via:

Twitter: @mba_cb

Facebook: www.facebook.com/sameer.kamat.sk

LinkedIn: www.linkedin.com/in/mbacrystalball

Email: info@mbacrystalball.com

I hope you do well in your life and your career. It's a small world. So let's not rule out the possibility of our paths crossing again. Good luck!

Appendix N
MBA Clichés and What They Really Mean

The MBA changed my life
A fantastic career, a great social life and a healthy bank balance…three of the things I had *before* I started the programme.

The MBA was like drinking from a fire hose
No matter how thirsty you are, I do not think it is a good idea to approach the fire brigade to quench your thirst.

Let's take it offline
I do not have the evidence or statistics to back up my point and it would be humiliating to accept defeat right now.

Our best assets are our people
Some of our people have the best assets.

Think global, act local
There is no guarantee our concepts will work within the country or outside, but they sound really impressive.

You gotta push the envelope
…yup, the pink one, to seventy employees as part of our cost-cutting programme…as I do not have the gall to do it myself.

Think outside the box
The computer is a box. The human brain is usually located outside this box. Don't be overdependent on the computer to solve all your problems.

The ball is in your court
…and so is the ultimate responsibility, the inevitable blame and the impending doom.
Corollary 1 – 'Your foot is in your mouth.'
Corollary 2 – 'Your balls are now in my court.' (Implied message from manager to new employee on the day of joining.)

Optimizing the value chain
Outsourcing.

See the big picture
Let's go to the movies. Work sucks.

Tick in the box
I don't care if the underlying problem has been addressed. As long as you can temporarily knock it off the list, you are still in the running for that promotion.

Best practices
Those arcane, outdated and impractical suggestions that the high-flying team of consultants copied from their standard repository and delivered to us, without really understanding our business.

Back to the drawing board
The six-month time period between getting your fantastic sounding proposal shot down in broad daylight in front of all your colleagues and walking towards the boardroom with your new improved proposal, knowing well that it would meet a similar fate in an hour's time.

At the end of the day…
…I want to go home and sleep in peace.